£9.99

turning the page

Barbara Hume and Richard Smi

D1335781

Acknowledgements

The authors and publishers would like to thank the staff and children of East Sheen Primary School and Trafalgar Junior School, for their support and contributions of work during the preparation of this book. They would also like to give thanks to Tony West for his advice and assistance, and to Bryony Smith for her artistic contributions.

Line drawings by Glenn Goodwin

Title panels by Brian Lee (Graham-Cameron illustration)

First Published in 1998 by
BELAIR PUBLICATIONS LIMITED
Albert House, Apex Business Centre, Boscombe Road, Dunstable, Beds LU5 4RL
© 1998 Barbara Hume and Richard Smith
Editor Robyn Gordon
Designed by Lynn Hooker
Photography by Kelvin Freeman
ISBN 0 947882 84 7
Printed in
Hong Kong through Word Print

Contents

THE READING ENVIRONMENT

Within a school the 'reading environment' in which the children find themselves exists on a number of levels: from the broadest - the school's ethos and organisation of reading; to the narrowest - a child with a book.

The broader issues are those of school policy: how reading is taught and promoted, and how books and teaching materials are organized and used. However, they can also be less tangible, such as, for example, the school's attitude to the world of books and reading and how that is expressed within the school community. Children are not just learning the skills of reading, but understanding the importance of those skills, the pleasure reading can bring and the worlds of information it can give them access to. In a school where there is a 'buzz about books', many aspects of reading will be made easier: the ability to make appropriate choices, knowledge about what is available and, above all, the desire to become a true reader who not only can, but does read.

The majority of this book will be about how individual teachers working in the classroom can help to develop the children's reading skills and knowledge about books and can convince them of the value and pleasure that can follow. However, it is worth looking first at some *whole-school* measures that can create the right ethos and prepare the foundations for the teaching of reading.

A school where reading is truly valued should contain the following:

- a wide selection of reading material appropriate for all levels of ability
- an attractive, user–friendly library, containing fiction and non–fiction
- books which are very accessible to children and teachers
- a common approach to reading, understood by the whole school community
- books and stories as a part of everyday school life – in different curriculum areas, on school journeys, and so on
- a programme of book-related events - from visiting authors to book fairs; from second-hand book sales to quizzes

- imaginative and eye-catching displays around themes connected with books or involving books as part of the display

- timetabling that shows reading as a high status activity - with regular library sessions, shared and guided reading lessons, and opportunities for individual quiet reading and whole class story

- teachers with a wide knowledge and love of children's books and the ability to share their enthusiasm.

Of course, a list such as this can be daunting and depends on sufficient funding and appropriate accommodation. However, it is good to have an ideal to aim for, and there can be little doubt that such a school reading environment would provide an excellent context for the work of the individual teacher and a high level of motivation for the children.

While these features do require a whole school approach, they make possible, and are in turn reflected in, the work of the teacher in the classroom.

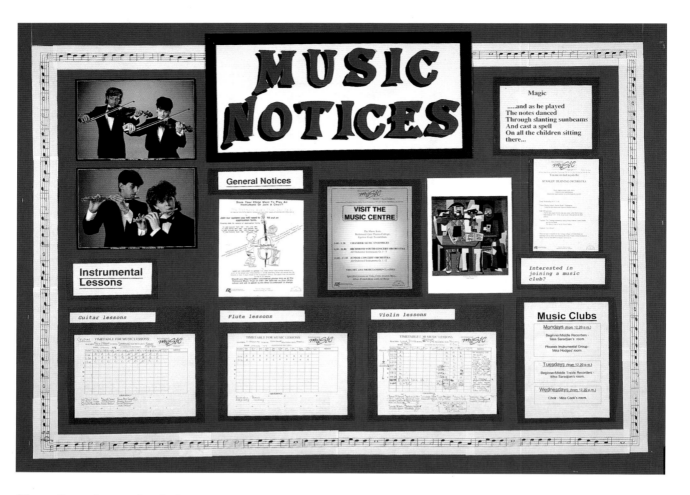

Non-book material

In the school environment, as in the world at large, children are surrounded by print. The reading of notices, instructions, lists, computer screens, advertisements, newspapers, comics, magazines, signs and labels, etc., are part of our everyday reading experience. This breadth of material should not only be recognized, but also utilized as a reading resource in the school.

The opportunity - or, in some cases, the necessity - to read this range of texts can be a powerful motivator, as well as showing another context in which reading in the outside world is essential.

The implications of this in the school are many. The following list provides some practical suggestions for considering these aspects of reading:

- Signs around the school should be clearly written and in language that is appropriate for the children.

- Where possible, displays should be interactive, with questions and titles that demand to be read.

- Written instructions for activities should be produced where possible: for example, next to the computer, where resources are stored, for games, etc.

- Notice boards should be used as a source of information, and the quality of the displayed notices ensured.

- Where appropriate, children should be encouraged to read school/home communications themselves; for example, school newsletters, letters about trips.

THE CLASSROOM READING ENVIRONMENT

The role of the teacher in creating a stimulating environment for reading within the classroom cannot be over-emphasized. The enthusiasm and interest that the teacher shows personally in reading will be directly reflected in the attitudes and responses of the children. For example, the teacher's own book collection displayed in an organized and attractive way will inspire and motivate the children and will indicate the value that the teacher attaches to books. The teacher can also generate informal discussions about books and reading by introducing the children to new publications and by drawing their attention to particular authors. The reading of book openings and carefully selected extracts by the teacher is another strategy that can be used to encourage children to read independently.

- The classroom book corner or reading area should be clearly demarcated and sectioned off from the rest of the room but, if space is limited, does not necessarily have to be large. Partitions can be created by enclosing the area using a display board or screen, or a bookcase or book-box turned at right angles to the wall. Areas can be created by draping fabric or curling corrugated card around a table or bookcase.

- The area should contain some comfortable seating, cushions, a carpet, a table (for writing, note-taking and research projects), a tape-recorder, and as much storage space for books as possible. The class computer could also be sited in the reading area, offering opportunities for the reading of IT-based reference materials. The process of designing the classroom reading area or school library could be undertaken by the children themselves as a design challenge.

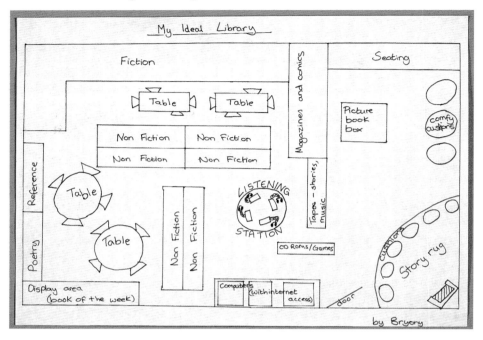

Child's floor plan for a school library

- Long shelves of books can be difficult to manage (to extract or replace books and to keep them upright), so it is suggested that a system of sectioning books is devised either using commercially-produced dividers, or by storing books in small plastic containers (such as kitchen storage containers, or plastic window boxes). Magazines can be stored in A4 files or storage boxes. Magazines and booklets can also be successfully stored by threading them with string and pinning them to a board.

- Ensure that as many books as possible are displayed facing the front. If angled display shelving is not available, then traditional shelving can be adapted by gluing or tacking wooden beading to the front edge of the shelf to provide support for the books. Paperback books should be covered - the easiest and most cost-effective method is to buy adjustable plastic jackets that can be re-used.

- Establish class rules with the children to maintain a good working atmosphere in the reading area, and respect for equipment and resources.

- Involve the children in creating the classroom book collection. Find out what they are reading outside school and ask them to suggest additions for class and school libraries. Book catalogues and book reviews from newspapers and magazines can also be placed in the class reading area, inviting children to read and make their own responses.

- The reading resources should include a wide range of texts and materials catering for the span of ability and reading proficiency within the class, and reflecting the interests of the children. The classroom collection should include:
    - play scripts (multiple copies stored in plastic zip folders – labelled with information about the number of characters featured, and some indication of reading level)
    - newspapers – national and local
    - magazines – children's and special interest
    - dictionaries and thesauruses
    - encyclopaedias
    - atlases
    - modern fiction – to include a wide range of genres

- classics
- traditional stories
- modern and classic poetry
- bi–lingual texts
- myths and legends
- a wide range of non–fiction
- picture books
- puzzle, games and activity books
- good quality graded reading materials by recognized authors
- catalogues and posters explaining the classification system used within the school
- taped stories and CD-Rom books.

In choosing books for the classroom collection, care should be taken to ensure that both fiction and non-fiction texts portray people in a variety of settings and communities, and reflect a multi-cultural society.

The children's interest in the classroom collection can be maintained and developed by the creation of a series of thematic displays and book-related activities. Interactive displays incorporating features such as research challenges or quizzes can stimulate and renew the children's enthusiasm for reading and responding to literature. At a simple level, the display could focus on the current class topic and could feature a collection of fiction, poetry and non-fiction texts relating to the theme.

Alternatively, the focus could be:
- an author's work - featuring the 'author of the week'
- a genre - such as science fiction, animal stories, school stories, horror, mystery, historical fiction, autobiography and biography, picture books, or stories featured in recent films and television programmes
- a collection of poetry books including both modern and classic texts
- a collection of newspapers, magazines or comics

- a display of books written and illustrated by the children
- a collection of current favourite books based on data collected by the children throughout the class or school
- a collection of stories and books enjoyed by the children's parents when they were at school. Compare their choices with those of the children.

Special collections such as these can be stored in plastic containers and shared with other classes in the school.

Wall displays in the reading area can also stimulate interest in the classroom collection. For example, the children could be asked to identify a book by reading the opening lines, by identifying a description of a problem or issue, or by recognizing a description of a character.

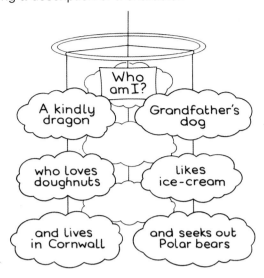

Further ideas for displays in the reading area:

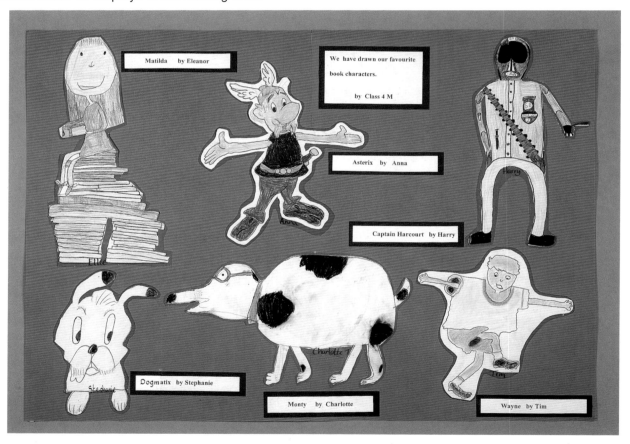

- a portrait gallery of favourite characters
- maps of story settings
- set designs for dramatisation of stories
- cartoons/storyboards depicting the plots of favourite tales
- promotional posters for well-known books designed by the children
- an alphabet frieze of famous authors
- a poster showing the class 'Top Twenty Favourite Books'.

READING STRATEGIES AND SKILLS

The need for the development of knowledge about words and the practising of phonic skills, the building up of a sight vocabulary, and the use of contextual cues to decode, does not stop at the age of seven. Competent and experienced readers continue to need to develop strategies for working out the meaning of text, especially when they are required to carry out the majority of their reading independently.

Teachers need to assess each child's use of reading strategies in order to develop an effective reading programme for individual children, and appropriate schemes of work for groups within the class.

Firstly, the teacher needs to consider:
What do skilled, independent and reflective readers need to be able to do?

- to be able to choose their own reading material, and to justify their personal choice
- to be able to read silently with fluency and understanding
- to read with expression and intonation when reading aloud
- to be able to self-correct and to re-read to maintain meaning
- to be able to recall and retell the plot and to discuss features of the text
- to be able to use a range of strategies to make appropriate predictions
- to know how to use non-fiction texts, and to understand how to use features of their layout, format and organisation to access information
- to be able to scan text quickly and accurately to extract information
- to develop a critical response to texts and to be able to express thoughts, feelings and opinions using appropriate and effective terminology
- to be able to discuss the author's use of language and devices such as irony for effect
- to have gained knowledge of grammar and syntax - how language works
- to be able to read and use punctuation for expression and to maintain meaning
- to be able to use contextual cues and the general meaning of a passage to work out new words
- to have built up an extensive sight vocabulary of common words
- to have developed knowledge of phonic patterns and letter strings.

The assessment of children's reading attainment and skills should lead to the identification of strategies and skills that need to be taught and learnt, and should give rise to the formulation of clear and precise learning objectives for activities. The teacher needs to make teaching and learning targets explicit to the children, drawing attention to the skills to be practised and developed. If the targets are realistic and attainable, this will lead to positive feelings of success and achievement.

INDEPENDENT READING

CHOOSING BOOKS

Although the aim for children between the ages of seven and 11 will be to develop them as independent choosers of books, their choice of reading materials will still need to be guided and monitored to ensure that texts are of an appropriate level of difficulty and that they offer both variety and challenge. In guiding children's choice of books we need to consider:

- 'readability' in terms of the vocabulary level used, layout of the text, size of print, language and genre, and the ideas contained within the book

- appropriateness of subject matter

- the range of texts chosen to ensure a balance of modern and traditional stories, fiction and non-fiction texts, poetry and plays.

Discussion about the child's choice of books can take place during both the informal, frequent discussions and regular reading conferences with the teacher. A reading interview gives the teacher the opportunity to review the child's past record of choices, to suggest alternatives and to extend the child's reading experience. It is important to keep an accurate record of books read, together with book reviews and responses to texts. This could take the form of a reading diary or log book. A tally chart is a useful way of ensuring that the child is reading a range of different kinds of texts.

HELPING CHILDREN TO CHOOSE APPROPRIATE READING MATERIAL

Talk to the children about strategies for selecting books. Encourage children to:

- read the back of the jacket - the blurb

- sample the text by looking at illustrations and reading extracts from the first few pages

- look up a specific topic of interest in the index of a non-fiction text and read the extract

- look for books by an author enjoyed previously and choose other books from a series

- take note of recommendations given by book reviewers on television or in magazines, or from family and friends.

Care must be taken to ensure that there are interesting and stimulating materials available for children who experience difficulties in decoding text. By listening to taped stories or by being supported by a reading partner, children with a lower reading age can gain access to more advanced texts.

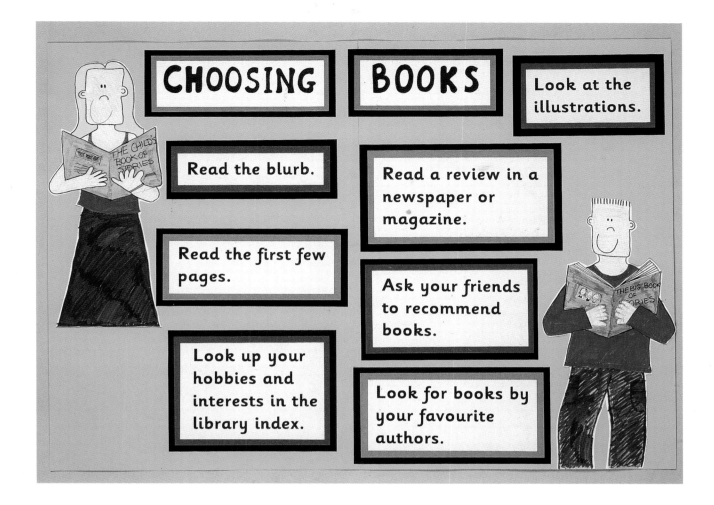

Activities can be devised to allow the text to be approached at a number of levels:

DEVELOPING UNDERSTANDING OF TEXTS

There is much more to reading than just 'saying the words'. Children need to experience activities that encourage them to think about meaning and respond to the text. These activities can take place from the earliest stages of reading development. A supportive adult asking questions and talking about the story or the pictures is doing just this.

In the past, comprehension often took the form of a passage followed by rather obvious questions, the answers to which could often be gleaned by identifying key words or phrases in the text and copying out the appropriate whole sentence.

There are, however, many activities that not only require a much more thoughtful approach leading to closer scrutiny of the text's meaning, but also are much more enjoyable and motivating. Through the focused study of one particular type of text over a period of time, children can develop a range of reading skills beyond simple decoding, and if taught with imagination and flair, can also develop critical awareness, an interest in language and a real love of literature that will stay with them for life.

If the work on reading and studying texts is paralleled by writing in a similar range of genres and styles, it is to the mutual benefit of both areas of the curriculum. By attempting to create written work of the same kind and intention, children will have a deeper understanding of the decisions made by the writers of the books, articles and poems that they read.

Equally, by reading, discussing and working on texts, they will become better able to match the style and language of their own writing to its intended purpose and audience.

TEXT LEVEL WORK

At text level, the children will be studying the genre or style in which the work is written, and the format and organisation of different types of text.

- In studying fiction and play scripts, they will be looking at aspects such as the motivation of characters, the structure of the plot and sub-plots, and how mood or atmosphere is established by the author. The children may discuss the theme of the book or play, and consider whether it contains a moral or message. More complex aspects such as a consideration of the author's point of view, meanings beyond the literal, and literary style, can also be explored in whole-class or group discussion of a shared text. There is the opportunity to introduce children to vocabulary such as: characterisation, setting, plot and sub-plot, theme, narrative, suspense, irony, menace, tension, inference, voice.

- The reading of play scripts will involve an examination of the organisational devices used and features of the layout, for example, stage directions, scenes, acts, settings, etc.

- The study of poetry will include investigation of different forms and structures, rhymes and patterns of language, rhythm and expressive, figurative language.

- In considering non-fiction books and written material, the children will be looking at the way in which the information is presented - organisational devices and layouts, and the style of language used.

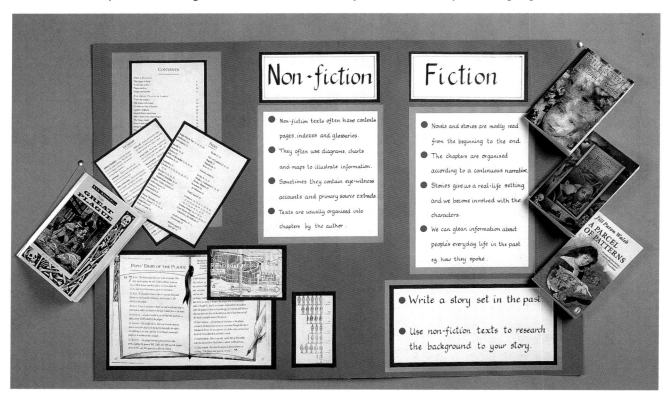

A comparison of fiction and non-fiction texts

- A whole-class or group activity may include the comparison of a fiction and non-fiction text: for example, comparing a novel and an information book concerned with the same historical period (see photograph above).

Work at text level that involves either whole class or group study of a common text will need specific organisation, as each individual will need to be able to read the text simultaneously. This can be achieved by using big books, multiple copies of the same book, or by studying extracts from a book enlarged and displayed using an overhead projector. The extracts chosen can be the opening chapter or a significant extract that carries the plot forward, or which illustrates a specific feature of the text being studied.

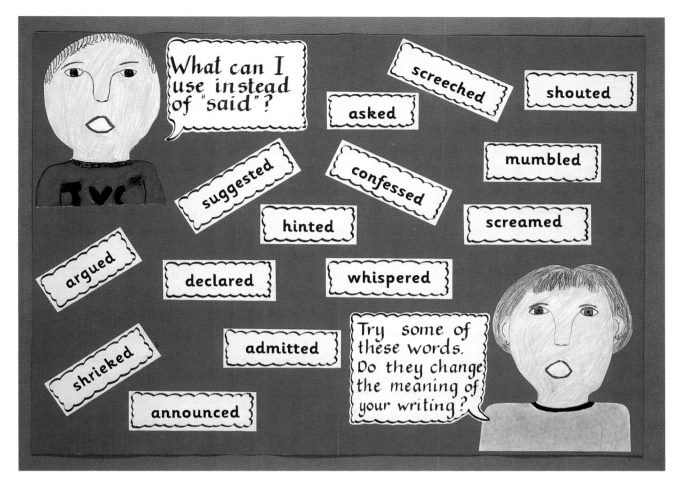

SENTENCE LEVEL WORK

At sentence level the studies will focus upon the way in which sentences are constructed and connected. Again, using text extracts the teacher is able to demonstrate and explain terminology such as *phrases, sentences, paragraphs, tenses, subject-verb agreement,* and *punctuation.* There is an opportunity to discuss word order, syntax, and the function of words within sentences - the parts of speech - using the terminology of grammar. Sentence level work can be carried out during both guided and shared reading sessions. Investigations and practice can be the focus for independent work.

Activities
- Sort and classify examples of particular parts of speech in the text extracts chosen for study.
- Ask the children to highlight specific words, for example, nouns, adjectives, verbs, adverbs, conjunctions.
- Make a collection of words and display these on a chart or a mobile.
- Adjectives can be sorted and categorized according to type, for example, colour, size, mood or feelings, number or quantity.
- Adjectives relating to a particular noun can be collected and displayed.
- Set the children the task of making changes to a text, noting the impact upon meaning and other changes that need to be made.

  For example, change: past tense   ⟶   present tense

                              singular   ⟶   plural
- Break sentences up into words and rearrange them. Ask the children: Which sentences still make sense? Which ones change the meaning? Which ones make no sense at all? Look at how word order is sometimes changed for effect in poetry.
- To investigate adverbs:
  - Play a game called "In the manner of ...." in which the children have to guess the adverb being acted out in the charade.
  - Ask children to write appropriate direct speech for specific characters, for example, "I don't think I can go on!" the actress exclaimed *dramatically.*

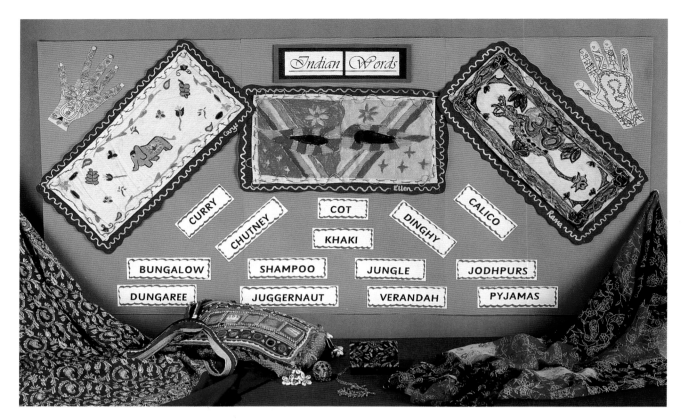

WORD LEVEL WORK

At word level, the focus is upon the individual words of the text. This might mean work on specific vocabulary, meanings and definitions, and an appreciation of why a writer chose a particular word for a particular context. Here there will be the opportunity to develop strategies for decoding unfamiliar words as discussed earlier in this chapter by:

- developing knowledge of phonics by using texts with recognisable repetitive patterns, rhyme and rhythm
- studying common prefixes and suffixes
- looking at how plurals are made
- identifying short words within longer words
- using syllabification to aid decoding
- investigating compound words
- looking at homophones - words that sound the same but are spelt differently
- exploring common spelling rules, and noting exceptions
- investigating common spellings with different pronunciation - for example, though, thought, trough, through, rough, plough
- developing and extending word recognition by studying topic-related words, making word banks and glossaries
- studying words with a common source. This can be linked to topic work - identifying words derived from, for example, Latin, Greek, Old English and other languages (see photograph above).

tele	micro
scope	mega
phone	photo
auto	graph

How many words can you make by using the Greek words shown here?

A display of books, artefacts and written work relating to a history topic

SHARING BOOKS

SHARED READING

'Storytime' has always been a common feature in schools, and while there is much to be said for the sheer pleasure of enjoying a book together as a class, it can also provide many opportunities for helping children to experience and appreciate language and literature.

Which books? Making choices

- Make sure that your choices cover a range of genres including, for example:

fantasy	historical fiction
picture books	ghost stories
fairy stories	books with a diary or letter format
myths and legends	books with a contemporary setting

- Discuss similarities and differences between books to develop greater understanding of the features of those genres.

- Choose books with sequels, in a series, or by prolific authors so that the children can go on to read more of the same if they have enjoyed your choice - and make sure more are available.

- Discuss reasons why particular choices have been made.

What's going on in this book? - Questions to develop greater understanding

Questions and discussion about a book being shared with the class can bring about greater understanding of the book, and also help children to frame their own questions when reading independently.

- Ask open-ended questions which illuminate the text and its meaning. Some examples that are generally applicable are:

    What do you think will happen next? Why do you think that?
    How does that character behave? Why do you think that is?
    How do you feel about the way that they behave?
    Does the author want us to feel a certain way about them?
    How does s/he get us to feel like that?
    Has anything like that ever happened to you?
    Does this remind you of any other stories you have heard?
    From whose point of view do we see what happens?
    What atmosphere does the author create in this passage?
    How does s/he achieve that?

- Encourage the children to back up their answers with evidence. This might be referring to a particular sentence or passage or to their understanding of how stories like this work.

- Give children the opportunity to consider questions like these individually or in pairs or small groups.

- Use shared reading to introduce some of the technical language of literature. This should include: *plot, setting, character, theme, dialogue, sequel,* and so on.

CLOSER STUDY OF TEXTS - 'DARTS'

'DARTS' are 'Directed Activities Related to Texts' and are an alternative to the traditional approach to comprehension, which has tended to consist of a passage followed by a list of questions which only require a fairly superficial understanding of the text.

DARTS not only promote a deeper study of texts; they can also be more motivating and invite a greater range of responses. Some examples are:

Cloze exercises

Provide a passage of text with gaps where certain words have been deleted. The children then have to identify words that would fit in the gaps.

- Children work in pairs - the discussion involved in choosing a suitable word is of great value.
- Discuss alternative suggestions - emphasize that there is not necessarily one right answer.
- Encourage children to identify how they selected the word. Did they use:
  - context?
  - understanding of grammar?
  - knowledge of the author's style?

  (The words deleted can be chosen to encourage the need to use all of these criteria.)

Mapping

Ask children to produce a map based on a description of the layout of a particular place.

Sequencing

A text is cut up and presented out of sequence. The children's task is to return it to its correct order.

Illustrating

Ask children to produce an illustration of a place or character based on information gleaned from a passage.

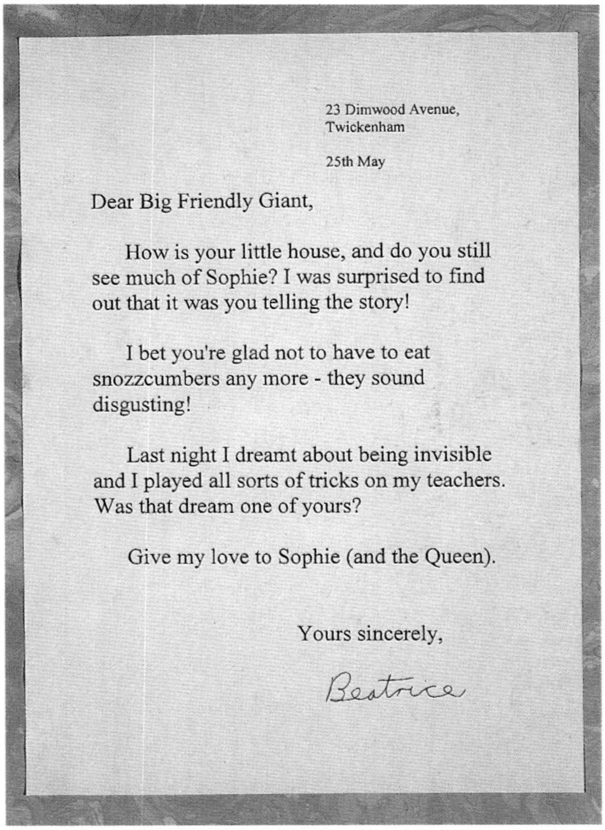

WRITING ACTIVITIES BASED ON TEXTS

Setting specific writing tasks can encourage children's responses to either a short passage or a whole book. These can take the form of straightforward book reviews, but more imaginative tasks can require deeper thought about the meaning and significance of the book and result in more creative responses. The form that these take obviously varies according to the book being studied, but some good general activities are:

- Write a letter to (or from) a character in the book.
- Write the further adventures of a featured character.
- Write a page from the character's diary.
- Write a story where you meet the character or visit the place featured in the book.

> 23 Dimwood Avenue,
> Twickenham
>
> 25th May
>
> Dear Big Friendly Giant,
>
> How is your little house, and do you still see much of Sophie? I was surprised to find out that it was you telling the story!
>
> I bet you're glad not to have to eat snozzcumbers any more - they sound disgusting!
>
> Last night I dreamt about being invisible and I played all sorts of tricks on my teachers. Was that dream one of yours?
>
> Give my love to Sophie (and the Queen).
>
> Yours sincerely,
>
> *Beatrice*

DRAMA AS A RESPONSE TO TEXT

Drama activities can provide an enjoyable and enlightening way of working with text. They can help children to experience events in the story more directly and to explore characterisation. The activities suggested below all require working from the original text and so very much focus on the need to read for meaning.

- A child takes on the role of a character in the book and other children ask him/her questions - which must be answered 'in character'.
- Working from a given passage, small groups of children prepare simple improvised scenes.
- A section of a story can be transcribed as a play script and performed. (This can work particularly well if based on a picture book and prepared with a specific audience in mind, such as younger children.)
- If a particular issue is explored in a book, a debate or 'public meeting' can be improvised, with children role-playing particular protagonists.

FICTION

Children should be involved with reading and studying fiction at all times during their schooling. This will involve thinking about their own personal reading, listening to and discussing a book read to the class over a period of time, reading and working on short excerpts from a range of books, and detailed studies of particular books. The techniques for looking closely at texts at different levels, which will be taught explicitly in whole class shared reading sessions, will become part of the children's repertoire of skills when listening to a story or reading independently.

Particular aspects of book structure and organisation of text can be studied and connections made with the children's own writing. Areas to look at should include:

Story settings
- Using the information in the text, children draw a map or illustration of the setting. It can help if children first highlight the relevant words or passages in a copy of the text.
- Children can collect evidence from the text that reveals the period in which the story is set.
- Children can imagine and write about a visit they make to a place featured in the book.
- If a story is set in a real time and/or place, children can research factual information from reference books and the Internet.
- Simple film storyboards can encourage children to visualize settings (see *Treasure Island* activities on page 26).

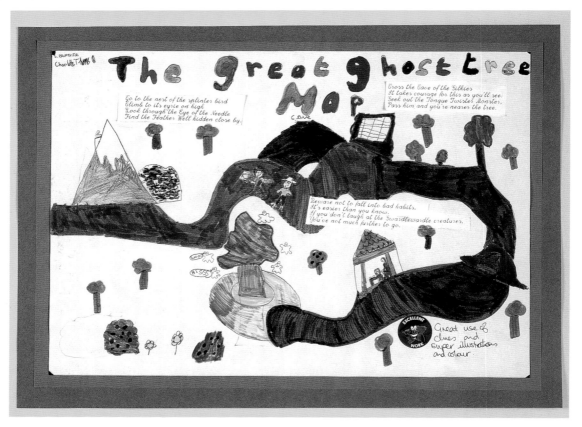

Story structures
- Plot the main events of the story on a timeline. This can be done separately for plot and subplot - or together and intertwined!
- At various points in a book, pause to predict possible outcomes. These predictions should be based on either evidence from the text or children's understanding of how stories work.
- Compare the openings of different stories. Which ones capture the readers' attention immediately, and which lead them gently in?
- On completing a book, look back at the opening pages. How was the ground laid for what was to follow?
- Graphs of the reader's emotions or responses can be discussed and recorded chapter by chapter. The emotions may include 'excitement', 'happiness', 'anxiety' or 'relief', and by studying them in this way it will be become apparent how the author builds tension or anticipation.

Point of view

Children need to consider from whose point of view the story is told. They should consider questions such as:

- Are we seeing the action from a character's point of view?
- Does this affect what is described - and how we feel about it?
- Is there an outside narrator with a global point of view?
- Does s/he comment on the characters or their actions?
- What does the reader know that the characters are unaware of?

In connection with this, study at word-level might focus on the use of personal pronouns - 'I', 'we', 'he', 'she'. Who is the 'I' in the story? Relate this to children's own writing, and the need to be consistent in the narrator's point of view.

Characterisation

- Build up a file on each of the main characters in the book. This can be added to as the story continues. A recording sheet can be designed requesting particular information.
- How does the writer build up a picture of the characters? Identify passages of text which:
  - are straightforward descriptions of appearance
  - describe the character's personality
  - tell us more about a character through examples of his/her behaviour.

Genres of fiction

Children need to understand that even within fiction a range of genres are identifiable. These include: historical fiction, science fiction, fantasy, ghost stories, fictional diaries. Genres such as fairy tales, and myths and legends, whilst not strictly fiction, can be considered alongside these.

An enjoyable way of understanding the features of a particular genre is to read - or attempt to write - a parody. This can work particularly well with fairy tales, where a considerable number have been published (see photograph).

EXAMPLE OF A FICTION STUDY

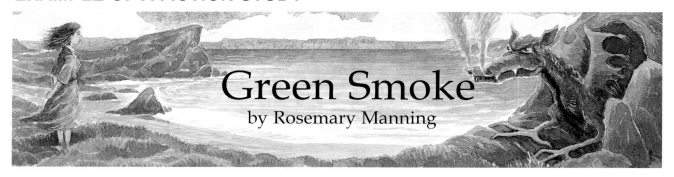

Green Smoke
by Rosemary Manning

Green Smoke is a charming, gentle book about a little girl on holiday in Cornwall, who meets a friendly dragon which lives in a cave on the beach. He has been alive for hundreds of years and tells her about the time of King Arthur, as well as introducing her to a mermaid.

CHAPTER ONE
The Puff of Green Smoke

This is a story about a girl called Susan, or Sue for short, who went for a seaside holiday to Constantine Bay in Cornwall. Perhaps you have never been to Cornwall. That won't matter at all. Just think of the rockiest rocks, the sandiest sand, the greenest sea and the bluest sky you can possibly imagine, and you will have some idea of Constantine Bay. At one end of it there is a high cliff with a lighthouse on top of it, and at the other end there is a great ridge of rocks jutting out into the sea. In between lies the yellow sand, and behind that, the sand dunes, with hummocks of tough grass, and little hot sandy paths running in and out like yellow streams. In fact, it is like all the best seaside places you have ever been to, rolled into one. Susan thought it the most beautiful and exciting place in the world. She had been there first when she was seven. Now she was eight, and she and her mother and father were just about to set off there again.

ACTIVITIES

- Working in pairs (to facilitate discussion and provide support) children can:
    - read through the passage with their partner
    - discuss their feelings about the place described
    - discuss any difficulties with the text.

- Read the passage around the class, following the text while others read.

- Hunt the adjectives - list them.

- Discuss the idea of 'superlatives' - there are many in this passage!

- Complete this table:

Adjective	Comparative	Superlative
rocky	rockier	rockiest
		sandiest
		most beautiful

- Highlight (or note) any parts of the passage that describe the bay.

- Use this information to draw and colour or paint an accurate picture of Constantine Bay.

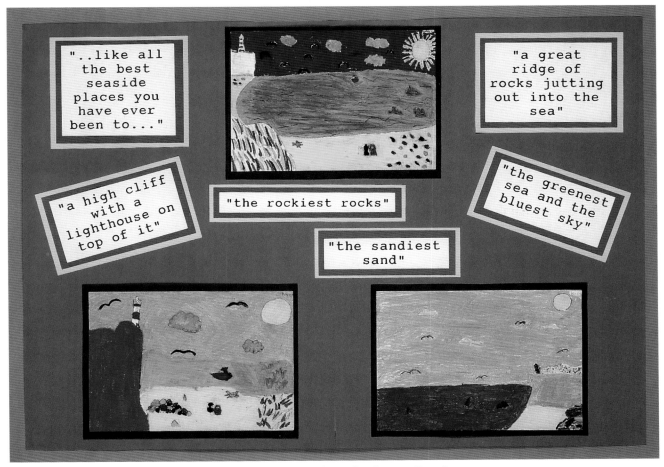

Pictures of Constantine Bay inspired by descriptions in _Green Smoke_

FURTHER ACTIVITIES

- Susan's mother thinks that Susan is only 'pretending' when she refers to the dragon. Children can write a postcard from Susan, where she tells a friend about the dragon, and another from Susan's mother, describing how the holiday is going.

- The dragon gives Susan 'dragon-charming songs' based on well-known nursery rhymes. Collect nursery rhymes and discuss patterns of rhyme and rhythm. Children can read nursery rhymes and adapt them to make their own 'dragon-charming songs'.

- Write a newspaper article or headline based on the sighting by holidaymakers of 'puffs of green smoke'.

- The dragon tells Susan lots of stories. Discuss the art of story-telling. Encourage children to tell stories themselves - either purely fictional or based on their own experiences.

- Collect and compare other books and stories about dragons and create a display with them. Children can read and review them. In what way is R. Dragon different from the usual legendary dragon?

- Use the book as a way into the Arthurian legends. Collect and read other versions of the stories.

- Use encyclopaedias/reference books to find out about the historical evidence for a real King Arthur. How can we distinguish between fact and fiction?

- Consider the idea of 'legends'. What other legends are there?

- Use an atlas to find the county of Cornwall in south west England. If possible, use a large-scale map to find places named in the book, for example, Tintagel, Dozmary Pool, Kynance Cove.

- Gather guide books, postcards and photographs of places in Cornwall.

EXAMPLE OF TEXT-BASED WORK

ACTIVITIES BASED ON CHAPTER ONE

Chapter 1: A Really Awful Start

• Write a sentence to describe each of the main events of Chapter 1. For example:

> Bill woke up and found he was a girl.
> He had to wear a pretty pink dress to school.
> Mean Malcolm whistled at him instead of bullying him.

• Talk about these events with your reading partner, or with your group and, after discussion, organize them into columns labelled:

good	bad

Discuss reasons for choices made.
Which incidents made Bill particularly angry?

• Look up the meanings of these words in your dictionary: *baffled, savagely, piercing, approvingly, glowered, snazzy.* What kind of word is *snazzy?* Can you think of some more words like this with a similar meaning? Use a thesaurus to help.

• Read the chapter carefully and draw a picture of what you think Bill looked like. Label your drawing with the descriptive phrases you have found in the text.

• What do you learn about Bill's character in the first chapter?

• Bill has some interesting ideas for alternative courses of action for Rapunzel to take. Look at the behaviour of heroines in traditional stories and fairy tales. Choose a fairy story that features a heroine and make suggestions for alternative plot developments and character portrayals. Read some published parodies of fairy tales to gather ideas.

• What do you think Bill Simpson would have said in answer to Mrs Collins' question at the end of Chapter 1 if the bell had not rung for playtime? How *was* he feeling by the end of the chapter?

FURTHER ACTIVITIES FOR *BILL'S NEW FROCK*

The following ideas represent suggestions for activities at word, sentence and text level for each chapter of the book.

Chapter 2: The Wumpy Choo

- Use extracts from this chapter to look closely at verbs. The children could carry out cloze procedure exercises in which verbs have been omitted. Look at the verbs used in the text relating to activities of the boys and the girls in the playground. How are they different?

- Bill heard lots of clues about the mysterious "Wumpy Choo". Ask the children to write these down, and to explain how Bill reached the conclusion that it was some kind of creature that needed rescuing!

- Use extracts from this chapter to show how dialogue is presented in the text, and how punctuation and paragraphing are used. Ask the children to list alternatives to "said" that are found within this chapter; for example, *scoffed, agreed, asked, announced, warned, yelled, explained, pleaded,* etc.

Chapter 3: Pink, Pink, Nothing But Pink

- Ask the children to identify adjectives in this chapter.

- Bill's teacher asked him not to look so gloomy. Ask the children to pretend that they are Bill's teacher and to ask him questions to find out what is wrong. Set the task of writing questions, remembering to use question marks.

Chapter 4: No Pockets

- Ask the children to list all the items that Bill was asked to take to the office.

- The yellow medical forms were in alphabetical order. Brainstorm the different situations in which items or names are listed in alphabetical order. Practise ordering names alphabetically.

Chapter 5: The Big Fight

- Ask the children to present the events at the beginning of the chapter in the form of a cartoon strip, sequencing the events and using speech bubbles to present the dialogue.

Chapter 6: Letting Paul Win

- Discuss issues of winning and losing. What does it feel like to achieve success? or to continually fail?

- Write an account of the race from Paul's point of view, or present the event as Kirsty (the best runner in the class) would see it.

Chapter 7: Happy Ending

- Write Bill's diary entry for the day described in this book. Record the times of the incidents, and recount his feelings and response to events.

- Ask the children: What do you think Bill has learnt during the course of the day? Do you think these experiences will have changed his view of the world? Explain.

STUDY OF A CLASSIC NOVEL

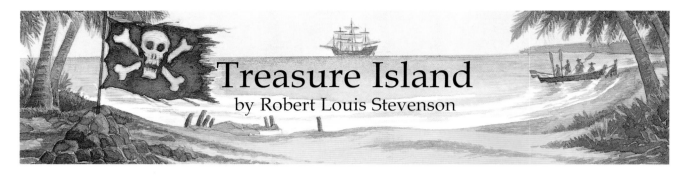

Treasure Island
by Robert Louis Stevenson

Stevenson wrote about this book: "If this don't fetch the kids, why they've gone rotten since my day", and its appeal can survive despite some difficulties with language and idiom.

ACTIVITIES BASED ON CHAPTER ONE
('The Old Sea Dog at the Admiral Benbow')

- Who is the 'I' in the opening paragraph? What do we find out about him in Chapter One?

- Collect adjectives and adjectival phrases from the colourful description of the old captain.

- Use the information in the text to draw a portrait of him.

- Study the passages where he speaks. Why are words and phrases such as these used? What do they mean?
    "a pleasant sittyated grog-shop"
    "Much company mate?"
    "this is the berth for me"
    "that head up there for to watch ships off"
(Relate this to a writing activity where children try to record the actual speech patterns of a contemporary person - perhaps a soap opera character.)

- Collect unusual words and phrases. Group them into 'nautical' and 'archaic' expressions. Do they all appear in a modern dictionary?

- "He would blow through his nose like a fog-horn". What other examples of similes can be found in this chapter?

- Compare and contrast the characterisation of Dr Livesey and the old captain. Pair up contrasting features:

Captain	**Dr Livesey**
"a filthy scarecrow"	"neat and bright"
"uses shocking language"	"pleasant manners"

- What atmosphere has been created in the opening pages of the novel? How has the author achieved this?

- Which characters might be important in the story that follows? What evidence is there for that?

FURTHER ACTIVITIES FOR *TREASURE ISLAND*
- Keep the diary that Jim Hawkins might have kept as his adventures unfold.

- Ask questions of somebody who takes on the role of Jim Hawkins and must answer in character.
  For example,

    'How did you feel when you first met Blind Pew?'
    'What were your feelings on sighting the island?'

- Scenes from the book can be rewritten as play scripts. Choose dramatic scenes to do this: for example, Chapter Five where the blind man and his cronies raid the Admiral Benbow.

- Using the information in Chapter Six, draw your own version of a map of the island. Some editions reproduce Stevenson's original. Compare it with yours.

- Discuss the role of women in the book. They are almost non-existent. Why? Does this make it a 'boys' book'?

- Use reference books to research the clothes, ships and weapons of the eighteenth century.

Film take	Treasure Island – Chapter Five	
Sketch	Event – Line references	Instructions
	'The Hispaniola rolled steadily...'	Shot of ship at sea. Sun setting.
	'It occurred to me that I should like an apple...'	Jim climbs into barrel.
	'It was Silver's voice...'	Jim in barrel, listening nervously. Cut to Silver, leaning on barrel.

- Make a film storyboard of scenes from the book.

TRADITIONAL STORIES, MYTHS AND LEGENDS

- Talk to the children about the oral tradition of storytelling and the history of the genre. Make a list of all the folk and fairy tales the children can remember. Discuss different versions of traditional tales, and talk about how variation has come about as storytellers embellished and adapted narratives to suit their audiences.

- Identify and discuss common elements and themes found in traditional stories:

   - a task, journey or quest to be undertaken
   - straightforward characterisation: good versus bad
   - a moral or a message to the story
   - the depiction of common human frailties such as pride, envy, vanity, greed, jealousy, and how these weaknesses lead to problems to be overcome
   - changes of state and disguise used as devices to advance the plot
   - danger, escape and rescue. Look at how salvation is brought about - by magic, trickery, or by an outsider
   - patterns of repeated actions in the plot, for example, Jack's three visits to the giant's castle, the granting of three wishes.

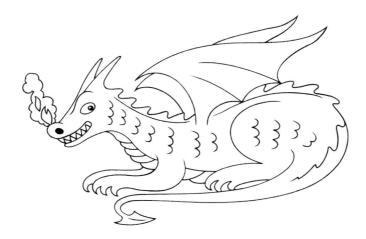

- Read a range of traditional stories from other countries and look for similar patterns and conventions.

- Read parodies of traditional tales, for example *Hairy Tales and Nursery Crimes,* by Michael Rosen (pub. Armada), *The True Story of the Three Little Pigs by A Wolf,* by Jon Scieszka (pub. Viking), *It Shouldn't Happen to a Frog,* by Catherine Storr (pub. Puffin Books), and *Clever Polly and the Stupid Wolf,* by Catherine Storr (pub. Puffin). Ask the children to write their own parodies of fairy tales, perhaps rewriting the story from the point of view of one of the characters and shifting the focus from the hero.

- Find examples of how authors use our shared knowledge of traditional stories as a sub-text within their own narratives - a device often used in picture books. Some notable examples include *The Jolly Postman,* by J. and A. Ahlberg (pub. Heinemann), *Once upon a time,* by John Prater (pub. Walker Books).

- Ask children to rewrite a traditional tale in the form of a newspaper report.

- Paint portraits of evil fairy tale characters to make a *rogues' gallery*. The pictures could be made into 'Wanted' posters by the addition of details of their crimes.

Theseus and the Minotaur
I peeked around my father's big gold throne and there, right before my eyes I saw 14 people. My father laughed in a cruel way then he, King Minos, said " Who shall be the first to be eaten?" Then a man I recognised stepped out in front of the other 13 and said, "I shall." "OK Prince Theseus." Two guards in red and black suits took him to the entrance of the big dark maze in the deep cellar. I dashed from behind the big gold throne to the entrance of the maze. "Theseus!" I called. He turned

around in an astonished way. "Here, take this ball of string." "Why should I, Prince Theseus, take this soppy old ball of string?" "Because if you don't you'll never find your way out again." "OK" he said, then he turned round and off he went. I stood in the doorway holding the end of the string. About ten minutes later I saw a figure coming up the stairs. "Hurry" he said all in a panic. Then he freed all the prisoners and dashed to the harbour. Luckily nobody saw us. It only took us three minutes to get there because we were all running as fast as fast

as can be. When we got there we climbed into Theseus' brown boat. " I'll have to come with you Theseus" I said. " Hop in" he said. So I hopped in with the 13 prisoners and we sailed off into the big wide ocean. Later on I went up to Theseus, " So how long before we get married then?" I asked. "Married?" he said, and he gave me a hard stare. About five or ten minutes later he sent me off to buy wine and bread . When I came back there was no boat. I looked around and then I saw the boat sailing away. " Oh well ", I said to

myself, "I'll just have to find a different man."

Cassie has retold the story of Theseus and the Minotaur from Ariadne's point of view.

Ask the children to write a story in the first person, taking the role of one of the heroes

MYTHS AND LEGENDS

- Talk about myths and legends - traditional stories of gods and heroes that offer explanations for natural phenomena. These stories provided ancient civilisations with a way of making sense of their world. To exemplify this point, examine a range of creation stories from different ancient cultures and identify common elements in the myths.

- Look at the language used in myths and legends, and stories of heroic deeds. Study the use of figurative language, similes and metaphors, to describe the powers and attributes of the gods and heroes. For example, look at extracts from translations of *The Odyssey* and *The Iliad* to demonstrate the use of figurative and descriptive language in Greek myths and legends.

- Word study could include an examination of the language of comparison and superlatives:

| fair | fairer | fairest |
| brave | braver | bravest |

- Examine the work of painters inspired by traditional stories, myths and legends. For example, *Bacchus and Ariadne* by Titian, and *Echo and Narcissus* by Poussin. Look at the devices used by artists to highlight the important people in the picture - light, line, and, in the past, the use of expensive pigments, for example, lapis lazuli. Ask children to paint pictures to illustrate a traditional story using these techniques.

- Investigate mythical beasts and creatures found in legends. Study the language used in the descriptions of these creatures, and ask the children to invent their own mythical beasts.

STUDY OF A STORY FROM ANOTHER CULTURE

Seasons of Splendour
by Madhur Jaffrey

This is a book of 'tales, myths and legends of India'. The stories are drawn from those the author heard as a child in India, and consist not only of the famous Hindu epics, but also tales particular to her own family. All are set in the context of the author's own memories of her childhood, which introduce each section and explain the importance of the stories within their culture.

The activities below are based on the opening stories in the book, and serve as examples of ways in which the text can be closely studied.

ACTIVITIES

After reading the introductory section entitled 'The Days of the Banyan Tree', ask the children to complete the following tasks:

● Identify the sentences which tell us what the nanny thought about the roots of the tree. (If given photocopies, children could highlight or underline the relevant sections.)

● Repeat this activity with the sentences which tell us the grandmother's thoughts about the tree.

● Compare and discuss the difference between the two views of the tree.

● Which view did the narrator agree with?

● Draw pictures to illustrate the two differing views of the tree. Be imaginative!

● Write sentences to support your illustration, stating which view of the tree appeals to you most, and why.

● What sort of style does the writer use in the introductory section? Why?

FURTHER ACTIVITIES
Read the two stories, 'Savitri and Satyavan' and 'Shravan Kumar and his Wife'.

● What is the significance of the banyan tree in each story?

● Can you tell from the stories how the banyan tree is considered in Indian culture?

● Does the story of 'Savitri and Satyavan' remind you of any other traditional stories that you have heard or read? In what way is it similar?

● There is a great deal of dialogue in the story 'Shravan Kumar and his Wife'. Rewrite it as a play script (see facing page). You will need to consider:

    - splitting it into different scenes
    - how many characters are involved
    - what scene-setting descriptions will be needed
    - whether the story can be shortened or simplified.

Kaliya, the serpent king, was no ordinary snake. He had five heads and was so large that he could crush humans to death in a matter of seconds.
The Serpent King lived under the darkest whirlpools of the Yamuna River.

The stories in the book are enjoyable to read in their own right, but would be particularly worth studying in the context of topics about India or within the wider curriculum.

- Build up a gallery of characters from the stories. Describe and illustrate them using the information given in the text.

- These stories are arranged in sequence as they might be told at religious festivals during the course of a Hindu calendar year. Find out more about this, and draw up a calendar of stories for the Hindu year.

- Gather reference books about India and Hinduism.

- Research the references to the characters, events and places described in this book. Do other sources describe them differently?

- Use reference books to find out how each of the Hindu festivals are celebrated. Are there connections with the stories you have read?

- Arrange a visit from an Indian storyteller or musician. Ask to hear their versions of these stories.

SHRAVAN KUMAR AND HIS WIFE

Cast: Shravan Kumar - An upright young man
His Wife
His Parents - They are old and blind and live with him
King Dashrat - King of Kosala

Scene: (Shravan Kumar's kitchen. He is sitting at the table with his elderly parents. They are all eating a meal.)

Father: Son, we don't want to complain, but we have this sour pudding to eat every day!

Mother: Could you ask your wife if we could have something else?

- The stories in *Seasons of Splendour* were told to Madhur Jaffrey as a child. What stories did you hear when you were younger? Are there any similarities?

- Make up a 'calendar of stories' for events in your year. These might include: New Year's Day, Valentine's Day, Easter, and so on.

PLAY SCRIPTS

The reading of play scripts provides an ideal and meaningful purpose for reading aloud. Group reading of plays encourages the development of skills such as reading with expression and intonation, and provides opportunities for discussion about characterisation, motivation and plot. The organisation for reading play scripts is also made easier for the teacher because the text is already naturally divided into parts. Care must of course be taken in the allocation of parts to children to ensure that the reading of texts is shared fairly and balance is achieved.

- Children will not normally be aware of the differences between spoken language and written dialogue. Transcribe some natural language from a taped conversation - warning, this takes a long time! Look carefully at the transcript with the children and ask: *Do people usually speak in complete sentences? Do they take turns to speak?* Compare this transcribed dialogue with a play script or a television script.

- Look at the features and organisation of a play script text with the children. Talk about how the playwright sets the scene and introduces the characters. How is the action carried forward?

- Find places in the script where the reader is made aware of the feelings and motivation of the characters. Do the characters soliloquise? Do they sometimes address the audience?

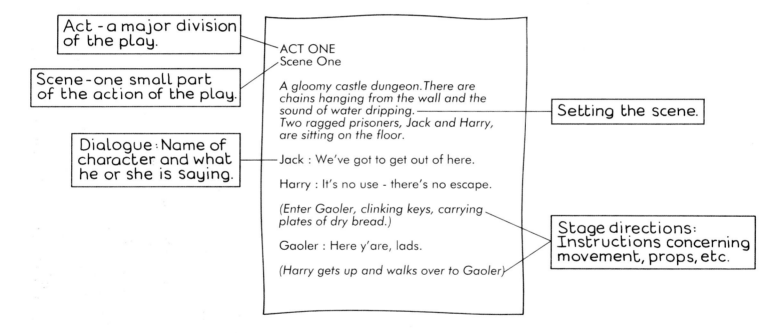

- Look carefully and discuss how the text is organised and structured. Introduce the children to specific vocabulary relating to play scripts, for example, *acts, scenes, stage directions, soliloquy, monologue, dialogue.* Examine how the text is presented on the page - punctuation, paragraphs, headings, the use of different typefaces, etc. Look at the language used - is it formal or informal?

- Choose an extract from the play and ask the children to identify whether the characters are explaining, telling a story, describing, arguing, expressing an opinion, interpreting a situation or the actions of others, giving a command, persuading, or asking questions.

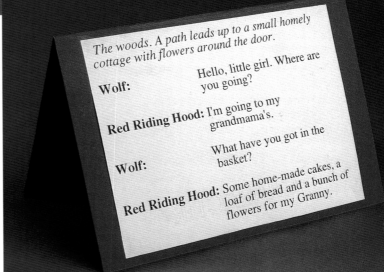

The woods. A path leads up to a small homely cottage with flowers around the door.

Wolf: Hello, little girl. Where are you going?

Red Riding Hood: I'm going to my grandmama's.

Wolf: What have you got in the basket?

Red Riding Hood: Some home-made cakes, a loaf of bread and a bunch of flowers for my Granny.

- It is only after much experience of reading and discussing play scripts that children will be able to write their own plays. Choose a familiar storyline or text in which there is a degree of dialogue - legends, fairy tales and picture books are ideal starting points. Identify a section of the story in which the characters might be discussing a problem or considering a particular course of action. Ask the children to write the dialogue for the 'scene' with a partner.

- Children can also be asked to write additional scenes for scripts using their ability to infer, predict and imagine.

- Listen to plays performed on the radio and encourage the children to perform a written script to be taped and presented as a radio play for the rest of the class.

- The study of Shakespeare's plays can begin with the reading of stories based on the plays. One recommended version is *Shakespeare Stories* (Vol. 1 and 2) by Leon Garfield, illustrated by Michael Foreman (pub. Puffin Books). Abridged versions of the scripts can also be read and studied in detail - for example, *The Animated Tales* by Leon Garfield (pub. Heinemann). However, children will gain much from being introduced to the original language and text of Shakespeare. Choose a speech or soliloquy and break the text into couplets. Look closely at and discuss the meaning of the words, the rhythm of the language and the ideas contained within the text. Give each child in the group a couplet to read in a performance of the script.

POETRY

Defining poetry for children is very difficult. The best way to help them understand and appreciate its 'specialness' is by exposing them to it. They need to hear it, to recognize its cadences and rhythms; and they need to read it, to appreciate the importance of how it is set out on the page.

Poetry can, of course, be obscure, but there is also a great quantity of accessible poetry for children. The concise nature of poetry can make it particularly appealing to those without the stamina to persist with lengthier texts.

Like fiction, poetry can appear incidentally in school life as well as in a focused study as part of a scheme of work.

Children should experience a wide range of types of poetry, including:

performance poetry	rap
narrative poems	song lyrics
ballads	shape poems
classic poems	acrostics
nursery rhymes	riddles
humorous verse	specific forms, such as haiku, tanka, cinquains and sonnets

Poetry in the life of the school

Poetry can be displayed in all sorts of places round the school, and its brevity and layout can mean that it will be read by the casual passer-by.

- Ensure that a range of poetry books are available in classrooms and the library.

- Poetry naturally lends itself to consideration of issues, wonder at the natural world, and reflection upon the spiritual side of life.

- Use an overhead projector when reading a poem aloud. It can be revealed bit by bit and the layout on the page better appreciated.

- Publish children's poetry in newsletters, magazines or class anthologies.

- Include a poem or poetry books in topic-based displays. This is easier with some topics than others.

- Read a poem a day to the class. (Appoint a 'poetry pest' whose job it is to remind you!)

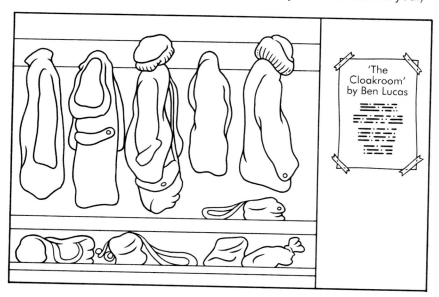

'The Cloakroom' by Ben Lucas

- Place copies of poems around the school in appropriate places. Poems about food can go by the school dinner menu, and playtime poems in the playground. These will need to be changed frequently for maximum impact.

EXAMPLES OF POETRY STUDY

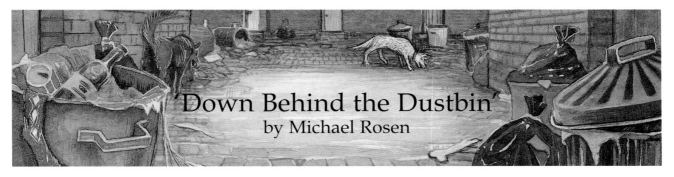

'Down Behind the Dustbin'
by Michael Rosen

This is a series of poems which follow a very simple formula, but can nevertheless provide the opportunity to look at rhythm and rhyme. Children can then have fun using this structure to write their own poetry.

SUGGESTED ACTIVITIES

- Read aloud poems from 'Down Behind the Dustbin' (in *You Tell Me,* pub. Puffin) - to get a feel for the rhythm of them.

- Learn them off by heart!

- Make up a tune and sing them.

- Clap the rhythm of the poems.

- Have a go at writing your own version. Some may sound better than others. Why?

- Explore the structure of the poems.

    Which lines rhyme?

    Which parts are the same in all of them?

    Does each line need a set number of syllables?

    How are they set out on the page?

- Write lots of poems in draft form. Read them aloud to friends - for comment, discussion and evaluation.

- Choose the ones that work best to write out neatly, and then illustrate.

- How could the structure/formula be adapted? Try to vary it, for example:

    "Up above the ceiling
    I heard a . . . .
    . . . .

- Read and study other examples of Michael Rosen's poetry and make a collection of his poems. Are the poems in 'Down Behind the Dustbin' typical of his style?

- Compare the form of these poems with the limerick form. In what ways is it similar/different?

The Listeners

'Is there anybody there?' said the Traveller,
    Knocking on the moonlit door;
And his horse in the silence champed the grasses
    Of the forest's ferny floor:
And a bird flew up out of the turret,
    Above the Traveller's head:
And he smote upon the door again a second time;
    'Is there anybody there?' he said.
But no one descended to the Traveller;
    No head from the leaf-fringed sill
Leaned over and looked into his grey eyes,
    Where he stood perplexed and still.
But only a host of phantom listeners
    That dwelt in the lone house then
Stood listening in the quiet of the moonlight
    To that voice from the world of men:
Stood thronging the faint moonbeams on the dark stair,
    That goes down to the empty hall,
Hearkening in an air stirred and shaken
    By the lonely Traveller's call.
And he felt in his heart their strangeness,
    Their stillness answering his cry,
While his horse moved, cropping the dark turf,
    'Neath the starred and leafy sky;
For he suddenly smote on the door, even
    Louder, and lifted his head:-
'Tell them I came, and no one answered,
    That I kept my word,' he said.
Never the least stir made the listeners,
    Though every word he spake
Fell echoing through the shadowiness of the still house
    From the one man left awake:
Ay, they heard his foot upon the stirrup,
    And the sound of iron on stone,
And how the silence surged softly backward,
    When the plunging hoofs were gone.

Walter de la Mare

'The Listeners'
by Walter de la Mare

Read 'The Listeners' by Walter de la Mare (see facing page).

Although difficult in parts, this poem is quite accessible and provides an excellent example for considering the creation of atmosphere. It has the *tension* and *frisson* of a ghost story - but the narrative is untold and can only be guessed at!

ACTIVITIES

- Children work in pairs to read the text together.

- Read the text as a class, discussing any difficult words or phrases.

- Discuss the feelings it evokes. Which parts of the text make you feel like that? How does the poet achieve this effect?

- Ask the class to formulate questions that they would like answers to. Compile a list of questions and discuss them.

- Explain the technique of *alliteration*. Can the children find examples of it in the poem?

- Silence and sound are very important in the poem. Collect examples of words or phrases that mention, describe or refer to them.

- Which words used in the poem are no longer in common use? What might the modern equivalents be?

- Why does the poet not give us more detail of the facts behind the story in the poem?

- Can the children write - or tell - the story that they think might be the background to the poem?

- Find - or create - music to accompany a reading of the poem.

- Discuss how the poem could be 'performed'. Could parts be split up and shared between different groups or individuals?

- Illustrate the poem or a theme from the poem to recreate a particular scene.

WORKING WITH POETRY

There are many activities that can be used within each of these modules as appropriate, for example:

- Cloze procedure - specific words are omitted and children work in pairs to discuss feasible words to fill the gaps.

- Present children with a poem which has been jumbled up. Can they sequence it correctly?

- Encourage children to learn poems by heart. This can be immensely satisfying and enriching if introduced sensitively.

- Ask children to present poems. They can be read aloud, dramatized, accompanied by mime or sound effects, or sung.

- Design poetry posters, where the poem is the centrepiece of appropriate artwork.

- Link reading poetry and writing poetry. Using a poem as a stimulus not only provides a structure, theme or style, but also necessitates a closer scrutiny of the original poem.

- Give children the opportunity to browse through poetry books and select and share poems that they like with the rest of the class.

- Listen to 'rap' and its use of rhythm and rhyme. Ask the children to write their own rap, perhaps setting it against a musical backing track.

- Rewrite narrative poems in other forms - as newspaper articles, stories or play scripts.

- Collect playground rhymes from parents and grandparents. Tape them or write them down. Are any of them still in use?

- Invite performance poets into school to present their poetry. How is it different when performed rather than read?

- Discuss the features of particular forms of poetry - for example, the pattern of syllables in haiku or tanka. Such structures can be enjoyable to use as a basis for the children's own poetry.

CHILDREN'S BOOK REVIEWS

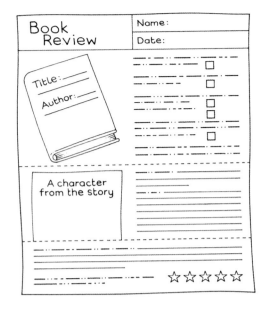

Book reviews allow children the opportunity to express their views about a story, poem or information text.

- Ask the children to illustrate their points by reference to the text, for example, highlighting instances of drama, excitement, tension and suspense.

- Instead of writing a review, ask the children to present a book report to the class. Encourage them to use audio-visual aids in the presentation and to include details of characterisation, plot, how the text is structured, how information is presented, the use of illustrations, etc.

- Set the task of presenting a review of a story or poem to the class relating to a particular theme, for example:
  - a poem that makes you laugh
  - a story that makes you shiver.

- Look at book reviews in magazines and newspapers. Read reviews of familiar books, and ask the children: 'Do you agree with this critic's point of view?' Ask the children to write their own book reviews in the style of the published example, perhaps making recommendations such as 'an information book appropriate for a seven year old', 'a picture book for a three year old'.

- Ask the children to design book jackets for books they have read. The jacket could include illustrations, a blurb or precis of the plot, quotes from reviews, and biographical details of the author (see photograph of Dickens book jackets).

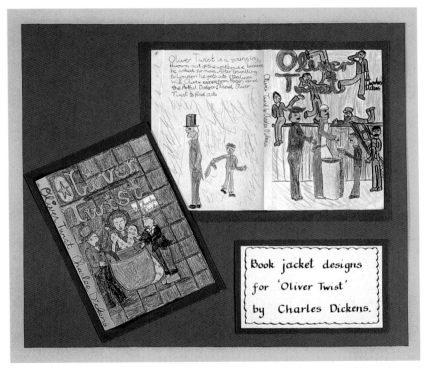

Book jacket designs for 'Oliver Twist' by Charles Dickens.

- Organise a 'balloon debate' in which each member of the group represents an author and his/her life's work. Each author then presents the case for not being jettisoned from the balloon!

- In shared writing sessions, write a 'frame' for a book review, with the children's help. Discuss possible headings, for example: *In the beginning.... What happened? To whom? Where? Why? So what happened next? The consequence was.... The story made me feel .....*

- Produce a class version of *I Like This Poem* (ed. Kaye Webb. pub. Puffin). Each child contributes a favourite poem to the anthology, writing an explanation and justification for individual choices made.

- Ask the children to design an advertising poster for a book. Discuss with a partner which features of the text you wish to highlight, and the information you need to give.

- Ask the children to consider: "Which six books would you take with you to a desert island, and why?" Talk about your choices and your reasons for choosing them with a partner.

- Choose two poems on a similar theme. Ask the children to discuss the poems, comparing and contrasting style and structure, the use of language and imagery, and saying which is the most effective or successful. Ask the children to give reasons for their preferences.

- Ask the children to carry out a survey of the books read by their teachers, parents and grandparents when they were young. Ask: Are some of these books still popular today? Read some of their recommendations and compare them with favourite books today (see photograph).

- Ask the children to write a postcard to a friend about a book they would like to recommend. Point out that there is not much space on a postcard, so words must be chosen carefully.

- Set up a 'reading circle' consisting of 6-8 members. Each child chooses a book in turn to be read and discussed by the group at regular meetings. This is an effective way of encouraging children to read books that they otherwise would never have considered reading.

Teachers need to be aware that the reading of non-fiction texts can be much more difficult than reading fiction. Reading for information presents a far greater challenge for young readers and requires the learning of quite specific new skills. Children are more familiar with the structure and language of fiction, where stories are read from the beginning to the end, divided into chapters, and generally written in the past tense using everyday, informal language. They have had a wide experience of having stories told or read to them, and indeed have usually learned to read independently using fiction texts.

Young readers therefore need to learn about the features of non-fiction materials, how to read them, and how to access and interpret the information they are seeking.

- Make a collection of non-fiction texts including:
  - text books/information books
  - dictionaries
  - encyclopaedias
  - thesauruses
  - atlases
  - newspaper articles
  - magazines, brochures
  - instruction manuals
  - recipes
  - diaries, journals
  - maps
  - rules, e.g. for a game
  - directions
  - advertising materials, posters, charts
  - CD-Rom reference material.

- Choose a selection of different texts, and examine their features with groups or the whole class by using big books, enlarged extracts, or by demonstrating pages using an overhead projector. Build up and encourage a critical response to the text by asking questions:

  - How successful is the text at presenting information?
  - Is the layout interesting and attractive?
  - What devices are used to make the information accessible (e.g. headwords, list of contents, index, diagrams)?
  - How are illustrations and diagrams used to impart information and to clarify points?
  - Look at features of the layout. Are lists or numbered points used to emphasize ideas, or is the text written in continuous prose?
  - Does the text lead to extended study by cross-referencing, by suggesting further research or reading?
  - Look at the use and purpose of different fonts, underlining, bold text, boxes and paragraphing.
  - What kind of writing or language is used? Is the text *explaining, telling a narrative (recounting), reporting, instructing, persuading* or *discussing different points of view?*
  - What tense is used predominantly?
  - Who is speaking? Introduce the concept of 'person'.

- For example, a diary is usually written in the past tense and tells a narrative using the first person *(I...)*. A recipe or instruction manual is organized in chronological order - *'first, next..., then...., finally...'* - and gives commands (imperative). History books and newspaper editorials can often present different arguments or points of view using the present tense and terms such as *'some people think...', 'because...', 'however....'.*

- Read non-fiction texts to the class on a regular basis, reflecting upon what has been read. Ask questions about the text and extract salient points. Teach the children note-taking by acting as a scribe, and so providing a model.

- Teach the children how to use an index, a contents page, a glossary and chapter headings to access information quickly and directly. Instruction could be given on how to use these organisational features using big books, or enlarged excerpts from the text.

- Carry out research as a class, group or individually on a chosen topic. Meaningful research, with a purpose, and within the context of cross-curricular topic work, will be the most successful in building up the skills needed. Help the children to identify specific research questions - asking "What do we want to find out?" - and discuss the key access words or search words to be used to find information.

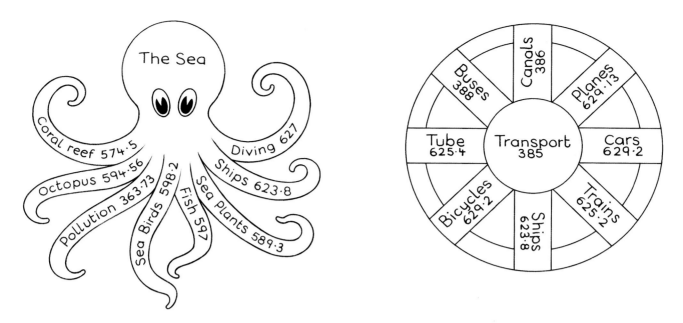

- Ask the children to design their own spider-graph diagrams to illustrate their research 'key words'. Display their designs in the class library (see examples above).

- Practise the skills of skimming and scanning text in shared and guided reading sessions. Organize the information collected on to a grid, poster or chart, and present it to the class to illustrate skimming and scanning techniques. Use the information gathered to devise a quiz.

- Practise alphabetical skills to locate information more efficiently.

- Teach the children how to use a library system and how to access information. Organize the classroom collection using a classification system such as Dewey. Visit a large local library to gain experience of carrying out an extensive book search using ICT. (Information and Communication Technology)

- Read original historical sources to find out about the past: for example, diaries, journals, the school log book, letters and eye-witness accounts.

- Look at how a particular event or issue is presented within a range of different newspapers, magazines and news reports.

- Investigate the lives of famous people using library and non-fiction resources. Present the information gained by writing a biography or by producing a 'This is your life' presentation.

- Practise writing instructions and make a manual (for example, on making a wheeled toy) to explain a procedure. Include diagrams and illustrations.

- Write a non-fiction text for classmates or younger children, using the information gathered from reading and researching non-fiction.

- Set up a class exhibition, gallery or museum and produce non-fiction literature such as labels for exhibits, brochures and plans.

- Make a 'goody' bag for a friend or relative based upon a particular interest or hobby. The decorated bag could contain a novel or story about football, a badge or rosette, stickers, match programmes, models or pictures of players, and a fact-file about a favourite team.

EXAMPLES OF NON-FICTION STUDY

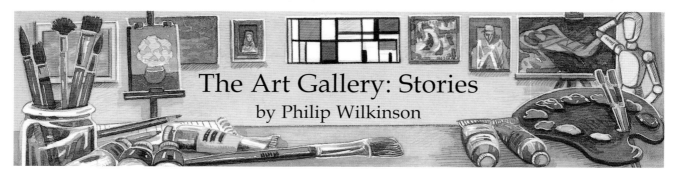

The two books chosen represent different kinds of non-fiction texts, both in terms of style and organisation. They were selected because of their quality, but of course the activities described below could be applied to a range of non-fiction texts, catering for a range of ages, abilities and interests.

- Read the blurb and the introduction to the book. Ask the children to make an assessment of the book based on the information given on the jacket. Is the reader given a clear idea of the content and style of the book and the information it may contain? (The jacket gives details of the ten focus paintings, a list of artists whose works are included, and an outline of the structure of the book.)

- Set the children specific research information retrieval tasks by posing questions such as:

  'How do the artists emphasize the most important characters in the story?'

  'What techniques do the painters use to make their pictures dramatic?'

  'Find out about the artist Fra Angelico.'

Encourage the children to use the index and to practise the skills of skimming and scanning to locate specific information in the text.

- Examine the design and layout of each page, noting the position of illustrations, the headings and captions used and the organisational devices employed. Is there a pattern that is repeated throughout the book? Is it easy to follow, and how does it facilitate the finding of information?

- Carry out further research about the artists and their work using encyclopaedias, CD-Rom/Internet and other non-fiction texts. Alternatively, set the children the task of researching the story contained within the painting. Is it a real story, a myth or legend? In which sections of the library are you likely to find this information?

- Present the children with a choice of postcards of famous paintings and ask them to select one of interest. Ask them to design and write their own text featuring their chosen picture in the style of *The Art Gallery: Stories,* for example:

  – to research the story behind the painting and to write a brief outline

  – to focus upon details in the picture

  – to research the biographical details of the artist.

The postcards of the paintings can then serve as illustrations. These pieces of work can either be presented as posters to be displayed, or can be bound together to make a class non-fiction text complete with contents page, index, glossary, book jacket, etc.

Think of an Eel
by Karen Wallace

- Read the blurb and the introduction. Ask the children: How do these invite the reader to read the book? Do they give a realistic picture of the contents of the book? Explain.

- Look closely at the text on pages 8 and 9. Ask the children: What type of language does the author use in her description of the young eels? Write down the similes and descriptive phrases used. Ask: Do you usually find figurative language in non-fiction books?

- On page 11, the text is broken up into short lines that emphasize the rhythm of the words and sentences. In what other genre is this technique found? Re-read pages 8 to 11 as if it were a poem, and try to tap the rhythm of the words.

- Compare the main text with the italicized commentary. How is it different? Extract the italicized text and read it continuously. Does it tell the whole story? Which style of writing do you prefer, or find most informative?

- Talk about the illustrations. How helpful are they in explaining the life-cycle of the eel? Ask the children to use the information gleaned from the text and from the illustrations to draw a labelled diagram of the life-cycle of the eel.

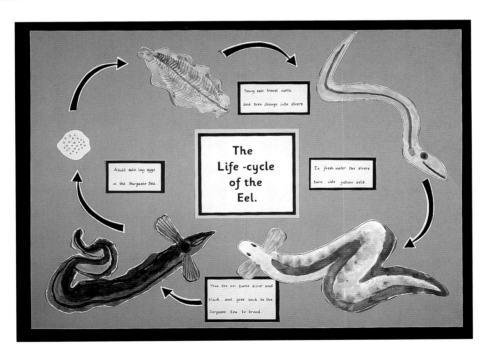

- Look at the way in which the author has chosen to organize the book. Compare the text with a checklist of common non-fiction features, for example, chapters, contents page, index, headings, sub-headings, glossary, diagrams, captions, etc. The author has chosen to tell the story of the eel and the account of his journey as a narrative - with the eel as the central character in the story. Does this text need to be read from the beginning to the end? Explain your reasons.

Children should be encouraged to read materials and texts in the world around them, and to develop an awareness of how powerful language can be in the hands of those who want to persuade us or influence our opinion.

As children grow older, they should be encouraged to identify the difference between fact and opinion; recognize objectivity, and how writing style and vocabulary can create hidden messages. Four possible projects are outlined here:

Signs, Symbols and Notices

This is an opportunity to use language in the environment as the focus for a study, and can give younger readers an understanding of the link between purpose and style.

- Go out into the locality of the school on a 'sign hunt'. Tell the children you are looking for examples of signs and notices in the environment (see photograph on facing page). Consider the purpose of the signs seen.

- Record what you find in the environment using cameras, sketchbooks and rubbings (using wax crayons).

- Compare and discuss your findings to identify the common characteristics of a sign (for example, clarity, short simple messages, bold lettering, etc.).

- Compare the variety of lettering used, and discuss the importance of shapes and symbols.

- Children can use their observations and research to help them in designing their own signs to go around the classroom or school. This can be a good opportunity for developing word-processing skills on the computer.

- Discuss the idea of symbols as quickly recognisable signs of companies or organisations. Make a collection or collage, including trademarks cut from advertisements in newspapers and magazines.

- Read and discuss the text of notices which give instructions, and talk about the type of language used. How is it different from a sign or symbol? Consider how far the language differs from a story or a letter to a friend.

- Children can write their own notices containing simple instructions for use in the classroom or around school. These might include: how to use the listening station, caring for the class pet, keeping the art resources tidy.

Newspapers

The study of newspapers can help children to develop a greater understanding of how particular styles of writing are employed in particular contexts.

- Use local newspapers as the core of the study, as articles are likely to be more accessible and of greater interest to children.

- Articles can be the basis for studies of newspaper language and, if photocopied or put on an overhead projector, can provide opportunities for the whole class to read and discuss features of the text, for example, headlines, captions, etc.

- Ask children to write their own newspaper reports about classroom, school or personal events, and try to get them to imitate newspaper language. This will give a greater insight into the features of newspaper language. (For more detailed ideas for a Newspaper project, see page 49.)

Fact or Fiction? Bending the Truth

This language project can work well alongside a history topic, where consideration of sources and evidence is important.

- Read and discuss two different accounts of the same event - perhaps a news story, an historical account or a sports report. Consider questions such as:

    How do the two accounts differ?

    What point is the writer trying to make?

    What words or phrases are used that show the writer's opinion?

        (For example: 'mob' or 'crowd'? 'riot' or 'disturbance'?)

- An enjoyable way of helping children to grasp the concept is to ask them to write a newspaper article about the story of 'Little Red Riding Hood', either for the villagers' newspaper, or for 'Wolves Weekly'!

- Read together excerpts from stories where the author's view of a character or place is obvious. Look for evidence of how the author conveys his opinion. How does he try to persuade the reader to feel the same?

- Use historical source material from reference books to look at 'evidence' and 'bias'. Examples might be:
  - conflicting accounts of a historical event
  - varying descriptions of a historical figure
  - reports designed to keep up morale (for example, propaganda).

The Persuaders

This is a study of the uses of language to convince or persuade people. The fields of advertising and politics, in particular, can provide texts for this.

- Read together and discuss the language of some printed advertisements. Identify the role of particular words or phrases. Are they:

informative?	untrue?
factual?	misleading?
meaningless?	designed to create a particular impression?

- Children can get a great deal of enjoyment from collecting and comparing advertising slogans. What message are the advertisers trying to convey about a product? How does the choice of words and style of writing contribute to this?

- Media literacy is not just about language. Ask children to analyse and interpret the visual images in advertisements. What impressions or feelings are the advertisers trying to convey? How do they achieve this?

- Children can have great fun devising their own advertising campaign for an imaginary product. This not only reflects what they have learnt from studying advertisements, but can also consolidate their understanding of the way messages are transferred.

- Politicians and campaigners use 'persuasive' language too. Older children could consider the arguments put forward on either side of a local campaign - by reading newspaper articles and letters. Having gathered the evidence for both sides, children could then conduct their own debate.

The media projects described above were chosen because of the possibilities they give for reading and analysing texts. Many other media topics could be planned, some of which may rely on a more visual approach. Possible topics are:
  - film and television studies
  - comics
  - children's magazines
  - the World Wide Web (see page 56).

NEWSPAPERS

Newspapers can be an excellent focus for reading study, for a number of reasons:

> They are a cheap and readily available resource.
> They use linguistic and organisational features which are quite distinctive.
> They are part of many people's daily reading repertoire.

ACTIVITIES

- Read and discuss a variety of short newspaper stories, either photocopied or on an overhead projector.

- Identify the main features:
  - headline
  - photograph and caption
  - quotations from people involved
  - opening sentence which summarizes the story.

- List the verbs in the stories. What tense are they in? Why?

- Consider the features of headlines, such as the use of dramatic terms and the omission of unnecessary words.

- Practise turning headlines into full sentences and vice-versa. What sort of words usually get left out when reducing a sentence to a headline?

- Working from a provided headline, write the story that could go with it. Be sure to identify the features mentioned above.

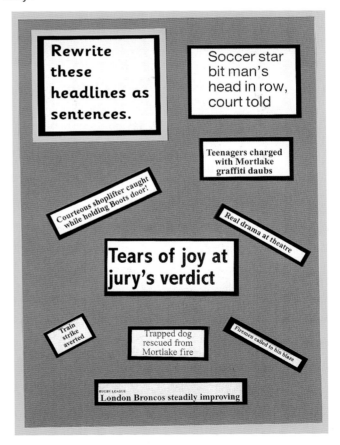

- Use a real newspaper report as the basis for text-based work. For example:
  - Find words that describe the people involved.
  - Rewrite the story from a different point of view.
  - Draw an illustration showing the events.

- Write a newspaper story in the style of a fictional narrative. How would the use of language be different?

- Consider the different types of writing that go into a newspaper? Make a list which might include:

  stories/reports   competitions
  articles   comic strips/jokes
  features (e.g. gardening) sports reports
  advertisements   editorials
  reviews   letters

- Analyse the contents of different newspapers to compare the proportion of each type of writing they contain. Younger children could work out approximately how many pages or half pages of each there are; older children could work out percentages.

- Create a class newspaper containing as many different types of writing as possible. If allowing children to research their own stories is impractical, give them a 'journalist's notepad' containing notes, quotations, etc., for a particular story, and ask them to turn it into an article.

6/12
Joseph Brown 10
Molly Keys 11
Cat on garage
roof
Children rescue
Ladder used

- Invite a local journalist into the school to talk about his work and to answer questions. Ask him to show how a story is developed from his notes to the recording of the finished article.

- Write newspaper articles based on other areas of work. For example:
  historical events
  story book plots
  religious stories.

- Focus on newspaper sports pages. How impartial are the reporters? Write reports of sporting events (national or school).

- Read a variety of published film and television reviews. What aspects of the film or programme are commented upon? How does the reviewer make his/her feelings clear?

- Write a concise book, television or film review.

- Collect old newspaper articles. Some historical issues have been specially reprinted. How are they different from present day papers?

- Establish a 'News Board' in the classroom where articles which have taken the children's interest can be displayed and discussed.

LETTERS AND DIARIES

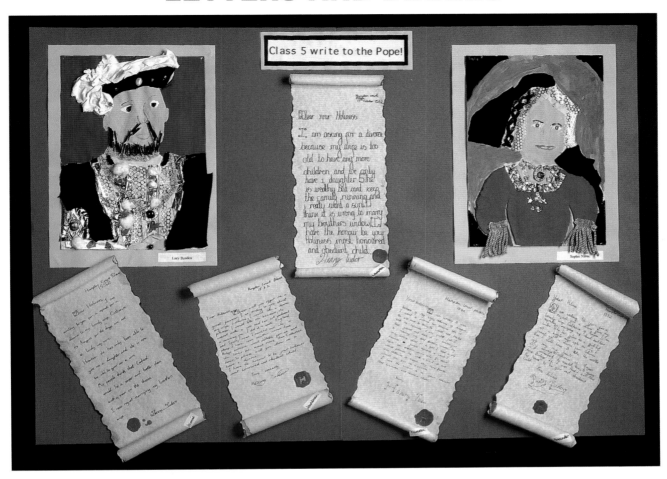

The study of texts in the form of letters and diary extracts can focus upon both real letters and diaries or upon those used in fictional works as a device to relate a narrative. Discuss with the children some of the main features of such texts. For example, letters and diaries can give the reader direct access to the writer's thoughts and feelings. Sometimes there are 'gaps' in the narrative where the reader has to deduce what has happened from limited information given in the text.

LETTERS
- Make and collect different types of letters to include:
    mailshots, personal letters to friends or penfriends, job applications, letters of complaint and replies received, business letters, letters to a newspaper, greetings cards, thank you letters.

- Look at the intention of the letter-writer. Is it to inform, to argue, to complain, to persuade, to express feelings, to thank, to enquire, to make a request or to recount experiences?

- Look at the style of writing found within each letter and discuss the level of formality of the language used. Examine the way in which the recipient is addressed, and the manner in which the respondent signs off. Look at features such as the use of punctuation, and the use of informal language - shortened words, for example, *can't, won't, I'll,* etc. Make a chart, arranging the letters according to the formality of the language used.

- Ask the children to write letters in a particular style using the knowledge and understanding they have gained from reading and discussing examples of this genre. The class could write to penfriends, to favourite authors requesting information, or to the local authority expressing concern about an environmental issue. Children can also write letters in role within the context of their history or topic work (see photograph above).

- Look at fictional texts which use letters to tell the story. The letters can be studied at text, sentence and word level. Some examples include:

Letters from a Mouse by Herbie Brennan (pub. Walker Books) in which S. Mouse writes a series of letters to the customers of an office suppliers at night, and in the process thwarts a gang of robbers. The language used is very informal, and uses direct speech - unlike an official letter from Hayes Bros. Ltd. The letters are mostly written in lower case letters with little punctuation:

> "dear customer,
> this is s. mouse of hayes bros. ltd and the reason i dont
> use capital letters is i got short legs."

This provides a good opportunity for children to edit the text, using capital letters and punctuation marks.

In *Little Wolf's Book of Badness* by Ian Whybrow (pub. Collins), the Little Wolf writes a series of letters home to Mum and Dad. The author employs the comic device of varying the way the hero signs off to convey the way he feels:

> "Yours fedupply..........Yours tiredoutly..........Yours damply.........."

Play a game with the children in which appropriate ways of 'signing off' are invented for characters in story books in different situations.

The Last Polar Bears by Harry Horse (pub. Puffin Books) consists of a series of funny and memorable letters from Grandfather to Child - describing his expedition to the North Pole to find polar bears in their natural habitat.

NORTH POLE

LETTERS - THE LAST POLAR BEAR

When you have had a general talk about the letter, discuss these questions:

(1) What can you tell from this letter about the characters: Roo
    Grandfather?

(2) Near the end of the letter, he writes:
    "Tell your mother I'm sorry, but I had to go"
    Why did he have to go?

(3) Have you ever been to a zoo and felt as he did? Tell your reading partner about what you saw that made you feel like that.

(4) Imagine that you were the child that the letter is written to. If you could write back to your grandfather, what would you write? Discuss what you might say.

(5) Working with your partner, write the letter back to your grandfather.

- Children can also be encouraged to respond to literature, by writing a letter in role as a character from a story. Picture books can be used effectively in this way: for example, *When Jessie Came Across the Sea* by Amy Hest (pub. Walker Books).

DIARIES

Again, both real diaries and fictional works can be used to explore this genre.

- Examine extracts from the diaries of real people - both present day and in the past. Look at the writer's intention or motivation in writing a diary or journal. Consider whether the author intended the account to be published for posterity, and how useful or valid the version of events can be considered as an historical document. Look at the treatment and inclusion of personal details and preoccupations as well as the more significant events of their lives.

- Find out about your school log book (see photograph). These were kept by individual headteachers and often reflect significant events outside of school as well as describing everyday life within the school. Look for evidence of the character or personality of the writer coming through. Select extracts that show a variety of styles of writing - formal and informal. Look at the changing styles of handwriting.

- Study extracts from Anne Frank's diary, **Anne Frank - The Diary of a Young Girl,** (pub. Puffin Books). During the course of writing her journal, Anne's motivation for expressing her thoughts changed. At the beginning Anne states:

    "I hope I will be able to confide everything to you, as I have never been able to confide in anyone, and hope you will be a great source of comfort and support."

    The diary was eventually reworked and edited by Anne herself for publication.

- The loneliness and sense of isolation of the writer is a recurring theme of journals and diaries, both real and fictional. **The Ballad of Lucy Whipple** by Karen Cushman (pub. Macmillan Children's Books) is written in the first person like a journal, and also includes letters written to relatives and friends far away. The letters have such a long, hazardous journey to reach their destination that the writer describes letter-writing as "like tossing words to the wind".

- **The Wreck of the Zanzibar** by Michael Morpurgo (pub. Heinemann), consists of diary extracts written by a young girl in 1907 on the Scilly Isles. Again, the sense of isolation is apparent in her writing, for since her brother left the island she states:

    "My house is not my home any more. It's a place I live in. My island is a prison and I am quite alone."

    The central character, Laura, states that she kept diaries from time to time as a young girl, and had later thrown them away. The extracts contained within the novel, however, related to a time when...."for a few months a long, long time ago, my life was not ordinary at all."

- Ask the children to focus upon an eventful period in their own lives and to write a diary extract recording their feelings and responses to what was happening at the time.

EXAMPLE OF TEXT-BASED WORK

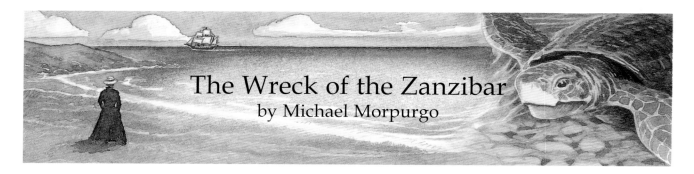

The Wreck of the Zanzibar
by Michael Morpurgo

ACTIVITIES BASED ON 'THE DAY OF THE TURTLE'

- Read the entry entitled September 9th, 'The Day of the Turtle' (pages 61 - 76).

- Plot a graph of Laura's emotions throughout the course of the narrative. Plot the high and low points and label them, noting significant events. As you read the chapter, write down words to describe Laura's changing emotions. Identify the thoughts and events that triggered these emotions.

- What does this chapter tell you about the character of Laura? of Granny May?

- What do you find out about the relationship between Granny May and her granddaughter?

- Laura talked to the turtle as she tried to rescue him. How did Laura try to guess what the turtle was feeling?

- What words or phrases does the author use to describe how Laura talked to the turtle (page 66)?

- Why do you think Laura didn't want anyone else to find her turtle? Was she anxious when Granny May appeared? Why do you think this is?

- Find a quote which suggests that Granny May is unhappy or worried about something in her life.

- At the end of this diary extract Laura says, "I haven't thought about Billy today and I should have." Is this true? Support your view with evidence from the text.

- Why do you think Laura wrote in her diary: "I shall remember today as long as I live"?

- What words or phrases does the author use to convey Laura and Granny May's excitement at their success? Look up the word *cavorting.*

- Write an account of the day's events from Granny May's point-of-view. Describe the thoughts and feelings that you think she would express in her diary.

FURTHER ACTIVITIES

- Throughout the book only a few of the diary extracts have titles. Is this significant? Look at the titled entries and say why you think they are named.

- Look closely at the entry for 21st July (page 39). How would you describe how Laura felt (for example, *desolate, isolated, lonely, hopeless, abandoned, imprisoned, cold, empty, suffering a sense of loss)?* How is this atmosphere established by the author? (He uses short, stark sentences with no embellishments.) What evidence is there of the effect that Billy's leaving has upon the rest of the family?

- What does this book tell you about the islanders' relationship with the sea? How do the young people feel about living on the island compared with the older people? How do you know?

- On 9th December Laura achieves her ambition to row out to a wreck in the gig, and her diary reflects her excitement. Imagine how Billy's account of the rescue might have read. Write an imaginary diary entry by Billy for 9th December.

- What devices in the plot does the author use to link the present with the past (the diary itself, and the figurehead, Zanzibar)?

- On 24th December, Laura writes:
    "Law of nature, she says. We saved the turtle and so the turtle saved us. It's that simple.
    You get what you deserve in this world, she says. I don't know that she's right."

What do you think? Talk about Granny May's theory with your reading partner.

INFORMATION AND COMMUNICATION TECHNOLOGY

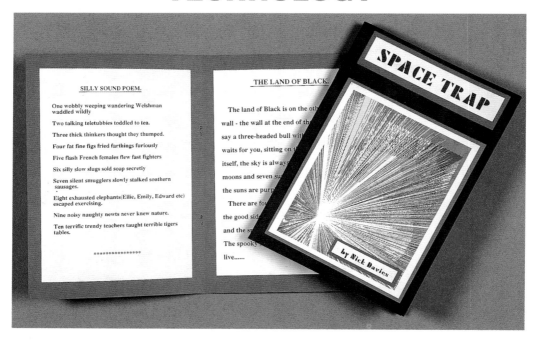

Whilst computers have for some time played a part in the teaching of reading, it is inevitable that national and global developments and increased provision in schools will not only lead to new opportunities for teaching literacy, but new types of literacy to learn.

USING PUBLISHED PROGRAMS

The selection of software needs to be done carefully, ensuring appropriate levels of language and, where possible, the need for a problem-solving approach. Organize paired or small-group work on the computer. The dialogue between the children using it will necessitate discussion of instructions and other on-screen text.

- Establish a bank of CD-Rom based fiction and non-fiction reference material in the library, and train children (especially library helpers) in its use.

- Encourage its use as an alternative resource to fiction and non-fiction reference books.

- Allow children the opportunity to browse through programs. This can encourage them to follow their own lines of interest and to find their own ways of exploring links between areas.

- Design specific tasks for more focused research using particular CD-Roms. Draw attention to characteristic features, for example, index, contents, links between one section and another, and on-screen controls.

WORD-PROCESSING AND DESK TOP PUBLISHING

Word-processing and desk-top publishing programs now facilitate the in-house publication of children's writing. This not only gives purpose and an audience to the writer, but also provides more channels for children to read and consider each other's work.

- Study different kinds of layout. Consider why writers and publishers have made the choices they have. Was it for the sake of clarity, convention or to attract attention?

- Explore different kinds of lettering or font. How do they affect the readers' feelings about the message conveyed? What fonts are available for the children's use?

- Relate the work above to the presentation of the children's own published material.

- Make books, magazines, posters, etc., of children's writing, and have these available for others to read. Add them to libraries and book corners, distribute (or sell) them to parents, and include them in displays.

THE INTERNET AND E-MAIL

Access to the Internet provides the user with a new and extensive range of information and communication possibilities. Whilst many of the skills needed to gain information from the Internet are the same as those needed to read any printed material, the nature of the medium does require the development of new skills, some of them obviously technical, but others which involve different reading strategies. The sheer amount of material can be daunting, and the ability to 'select and sift' requires quite sophisticated skills. However, there are ways to make it more manageable:

● Work as a class on the concept of 'keywords' and how to narrow searches down to filter out unwanted areas. Brainstorm keywords for a particular topic.

● Find sites specifically set up for children, which not only contain information but also teach them how to use the Internet within safe and limited confines.

● Download files where possible, enabling access without danger of losing corrections or straying into unwanted areas.

● Sites which have been found to be useful can be 'bookmarked' (indexed for easy access by children or teachers at a later stage).

● Use CD Roms which have the capacity to provide direct links with relevant sections of the Internet.

● Many children's authors have their own websites, as do publishers and booksellers. Access these to gain more information about literature.

● Many schools now have websites of their own giving information about their locality, recent projects and events. Individual children can provide motivating reading matter.

● Use E-mail to communicate with other classes or individuals. There are free clubs for children to make 'keypals' (penpals on the Net).

PROMOTING READING FOR PLEASURE

Schools can do much to promote reading as a pleasurable and worthwhile pastime. The opening chapter, 'The Reading Environment', outlined how an atmosphere can be created in the school where reading is seen to be valued. In this chapter we will look at the other ways in which reading can be promoted.

AUTHOR VISITS

Inviting an author into the school can be expensive and difficult to arrange, but there are many benefits which can be gained. These can include:

- a deeper understanding of the way writers work to create texts
- enabling the children to make connections between the way they are encouraged to approach a written task and the strategies employed by professionals (e.g. keeping a notebook, brainstorming, drafting, etc.)
- gaining a closer insight into a particular written text, by working with its creator
- the promotion of a particular group of books
- inspiring a greater interest in reading in general.

The type of activity that the authors will be involved in will vary according to their preference or yours: the number of children you want to meet them, and the amount of time you want them to spend in the school. This is usually limited by financial constraints.

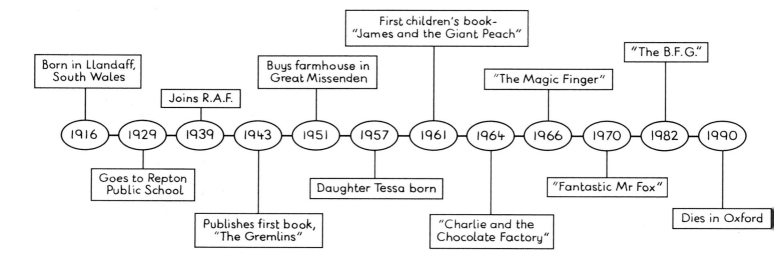

Example of a timeline based on an author's life

Finding an author

There are many writers who are prepared to work in schools, but their availability can depend on a number of factors, including the locality of the school and their own diaries (the most popular writers are often booked up over a year in advance).

There are a number of ways of making contact with them:

- Contact their publishers' publicity department. They will know about their availability and the type of activity that they like to engage in. If the writer you want is not available, they can also suggest alternatives.
- Writing directly to the author can be a shortcut - write C/o the publisher.
- The Children's Book Foundation in the U.K. publish a list of writers and illustrators prepared to work in schools and which areas they are prepared to travel to.
- The National Association of Writers in Education also publish a list and guidelines.

Using authors in schools

Activities may include some, or all, of the following:
- a performance or reading of their work.

- a talk to a large group of children about their writing - the process from original idea to publication. This will usually include a question and answer session. Authors often specify the maximum size of group that they are prepared to work with in this way.

- a workshop approach with a smaller group, helping to develop the children's writing skills.

- a longer term residency or programme of repeated visits. This approach can enable the writer to establish a relationship with a group (or groups) of children and to work on developing their writing over a longer period of time.

- a 'signing session' where the author's books are on sale in the school.

Preparation

All of the above will be more enjoyable, successful and valuable, for both writer and children, if carefully planned and prepared for.
- Ensure that the author's books are widely read in advance of the visit. Copies should be available in the library and book corners for children to read, and for teachers to share with their classes, either in their entirety, or using excerpts which will hopefully motivate them to 'read on'.

- The event should be well publicised in advance. This not only informs the children - and the whole school community - of the coming event, but also leads to an air of excitement and anticipation which helps create the 'buzz' about books and reading in the school.

- Displays can help to create this anticipation, as well as focusing children's attention on the particular author's work.

- Where the author is working in the context of writing workshops, it may be helpful to plan a particular project for the children to work on. Given the likelihood that the writer will have a fairly limited time with a group, some writing may need to be done in advance to give the author and children something to work with.

– On a more practical note, it is important to provide the author with necessary information well in advance of the visit. This should include:
- confirmation of agreed fee
- map details of how to get to the school
- programme for the day including confirmation of agreed groups and arrangements for lunch, etc.

After the event

Keep the momentum going! Take advantage of the children's increased motivation and provide opportunities for them to read the author's books, write letters of thanks, develop displays connected with the visit including photographs, examples of resulting work, and book reviews.

OTHER BOOK EVENTS

A whole range of other events can also be planned within school to show that reading has a high status and is fun. Some examples are given below.

School magazine

Produce a school magazine or anthology. Let the children see themselves as published writers too.

A Readers' and Writers' Club

This can be run in a lunchtime or after school and gives an opportunity for those children who are particularly interested in the subject to try some extra-curricular projects. Their work can be published or displayed and provide an extra stimulus for others. Teachers often run such clubs for music and sport. Reading could be given this same status.

Book quizzes

These could be organized after school for children and for adults.

Book character fancy dress

This can be great fun, but also helps to develop children's understanding of character.

Book-based discussions

Children's literature lends itself as a stimulus for thought and consideration of issues and children's views of the world. This not only brings the writer's imagination and sensitivity to bear, but also helps to put 'the book' (or 'the poem') in a position of importance.

Book Week

Organize a week focusing on books and reading. This can include many of the activities described above.

ENCOURAGING BOOK OWNERSHIP

While schools have a duty to make available a wide range of books for children to choose, borrow, take home and return, encouraging them to save up for, choose, buy and own books themselves is another aspect of becoming a reader that we can help to develop. There are many ways of promoting this:

- **Running a book club within the school.** There are many commercial organisations which can provide the opportunity to do this. It normally takes the form of leaflets offering a selection of books which can be ordered. The school can benefit greatly by receiving a number of free books in proportion to the numbers sold.

- **A school bookshop.** The advantage of this over a Book Club is that the selection of books can be made by the school, allowing particular authors or subject areas to be specifically made available at particular times, perhaps relating to forthcoming topics.

- **Book fairs.** Some organisations now offer a complete 'Book Fair' service to schools which involves delivering and collecting cases of books, and giving schools a discount to be taken in books. This can be a great source of extra books, as well as a means of bringing different books to the children's attention - but it can involve a lot of work!

- **Second-hand book sales.** For some families, the price of new books can be prohibitive, and organising a second-hand book sale can be an excellent means of allowing all children to own books. Books are donated by children (some publishers and booksellers might help too), and are sold at low prices.

READING CONTEXTS

SHARED READING

Shared reading is a class activity which engages the whole class in the reading and examination of a common text (often enlarged). There is an opportunity to teach children explicitly and model the reading skills and strategies which they require in order to identify particular features of a studied text.

GUIDED READING

Guided reading is an independent activity which occurs within a small group of similar ability children. The children read the same text, selected to be at an instructional reading level which requires some support and presents challenges that can be solved by the group. The children read independently (either aloud or silently) while the teacher monitors and assesses the individual's reading by listening, asking questions and setting tasks related to the text.

Questions to promote discussion

- What does the extract tell you about the characters?

- Why did they behave as they did?

- How does the author convey the characters' feelings?

- Does the extract give you a clear picture of the setting in which the narrative takes place? Identify descriptive passages and discuss any figurative language.

- Does this chapter serve to advance the plot in any significant way? Identify decisive turning points or important events.

- What do you think will happen next? What clues are there in the text?

- Does the author present a problem to be overcome? How do you think it might be resolved?

- Has anything like this happened to you?

- Have you read any stories like this before? Describe how they are similar.

- Talk about personal responses. Ask: How does this book make you feel? Does the author capture your attention and involve you in the narrative?

- Whose point of view are we given in this extract? Introduce the idea of voice and perspective.

Resources for group reading sessions need to be carefully organized in reading levels. Multiple copies of texts can be stored in plastic wallets, labelled with information regarding number of copies, number of characters in play scripts, etc. Details of suggested discussion points and related activities can be included in each resource pack, suitable for children reading at this level.

SHARING A BOOK WITH AN INDIVIDUAL OR A SMALL GROUP

Listening to children read aloud is a worthwhile activity in order to assess their fluency, ability to decode, use of punctuation, comprehension skills, etc. The opportunity for a one-to-one discussion with each child about their current reading book also provides further opportunities to question children about what they are reading and to encourage them to ask themselves similar questions when reading independently.

- Utilize the fact that the child has the text in front of him/her and can make references to specific passages to provide supporting evidence for answers.

- Vary the approach. If children feel secure they will be happy to read aloud in a small group - or to read silently to an agreed point before discussing together.

PAIRED READING

Paired reading can take the form of sharing a text with classmates, or reading with older or younger pupils. It provides opportunities for meaningful reading aloud and for discussion about text.

Reading with peers

- In this paired reading situation, reading partners take turns to read the text aloud. One partner could present a favourite book to a friend, and read excerpts to illustrate reasons for making that particular choice.
- Reading partners can also carry out cloze procedure exercises in which words are omitted from a prose passage or poem, and appropriate and effective replacements have to be inserted after discussion and agreement.
- The drama activity of 'hot-seating' is a useful device for exploring aspects of characterisation and motivation in discussion with a reading partner. After sharing a text together, one partner can adopt the role of a character while the other reader asks questions concerning his/her view of events, and about the character's motivation and feelings during the course of the story.

Paired reading with an older or younger partner

It is important for teachers and children to discuss and to lay down ground rules for reading with younger or less experienced readers. The older pupils should be given practical advice on how to support the younger partner's reading - both in terms of encouraging and suggesting strategies for decoding text, and also on the need for sensitivity in dealing with, for example, reluctant or hesitant readers.

- The older pupils can be encouraged to select materials for reading to the younger children, plan suitable questions to ask them about the text, and help them to read independently.
- The older, more experienced readers can be asked to write stories and non-fiction texts for their reading partners. This kind of writing for a specific purpose leads to valuable discussion and consideration of layout and organisation of reading texts, the use of illustrations, and the development of storylines, etc.
- The pairing of younger children with older pupils within the school can have further beneficial effects and provide opportunities for work in other curriculum areas, and in the pastoral life of the school.

ENROLLING PARENTS' HELP AT HOME AND AT SCHOOL

Parents can make a valuable contribution to their children's enjoyment and progress in reading by helping at home and in school. The school should emphasize and value the contribution made by parents, and should encourage participation by holding regular reading workshops and by publishing leaflets and pamphlets explaining policy and practice.

How parents can help and support their children's reading at home

- by reading to and with their children
- by joining the local library and participating in book festivals and events organized locally
- by being active and enthusiastic readers themselves and by providing their children with positive role models
- by visiting local bookshops and encouraging children to spend their own money on books
- by encouraging children to read in a wide range of contexts. Examples could include reading instructions, newspapers, magazines, recipes, notices, timetables, posters and packaging.

The Reading Workshop for parents

Reading workshops can be held at regular intervals to encourage parents both to read with their children at home and to come into school to support literacy activities. The workshop situation provides an ideal opportunity for the dissemination of information about the teaching methods used and the school's aims and objectives. Parents can be shown the full range of resources and reading materials available to their children, and how book choices are guided. In addition, parents should be given a written guide that explains school policy and that offers practical advice concerning choice of materials and reading strategies. An example of such a guide is given in the text on the following two pages.

In addition to listening to individual children read, parents can also help in school by:

- helping with group literacy sessions such as play script reading and group reading, provided that learning objectives and targets are made clear to both parent helpers and children from the outset
- helping to guide children's book choices in the library
- helping children to carry out research in the library
- organizing book clubs and book fairs and helping with book week events
- joining the school magazine editorial team and assisting staff and children in the production of publications.

LISTENING TO CHILDREN READ IN SCHOOL- A PARENT'S GUIDE

Thank you for volunteering to help in school by reading with children. The children will have already chosen their reading material, or the teacher may ask you to guide their choice from a limited range. Here are some questions commonly posed by parent helpers.

"What do I do if the book chosen appears to be too easy?"
Ask the child why s/he has chosen that particular book. Children will often choose books that are well within their reading capabilities to build confidence and experience reading as a pleasurable activity and not as a difficult task. In discussion with the child, try to encourage her/him to choose a more challenging text next time.

"What if the book is too hard for the child?"
Children will sometimes choose books that are too difficult for them to read independently and comfortably. Again, in discussion, gently suggest that something different may be more enjoyable, and help them to choose an alternative. If they are really keen to read the book, share the reading of the text, and suggest that they ask for further help at home.

"What can I do if the children get stuck?"
There are a number of strategies that children can be encouraged to use when they come to a word they do not recognize. Here are some of them:
- to use the context and general meaning of the sentence to make an informed guess or sensible prediction
- to use picture clues
- to use knowledge of phonics and common letter strings to 'sound out' a word
- to sometimes read on, or to re-read and to self-correct, in order to maintain the sense of the text
- to break a word up into manageable parts and to look for familiar beginnings such as *pre, re,* and endings such as *ing, ful,* etc.
- to tell them the word when, in your opinion, it will help to maintain the meaning of the passage.

"How do I know if the child has understood what s/he has read?"

It may be appropriate to ask questions about what has been read, and to talk about the plot, the characters, and what the writer is trying to say. Ask:

"What do you think will happen next? Why?"
"Why do you think the characters did that?"
"Have you ever met anybody like that?"
"How did this book make you feel?"

If the child has chosen a non-fiction book, discussion could focus upon how to skim and scan the text to extract the required information, how to use the Contents and Index pages, and how to summarize and take notes.

FINALLY, SOME GENERAL POINTS...
- Remember to take a rest! Decoding and reading aloud are both hard work, particularly for inexperienced readers. Offer to share the reading of longer texts if the child is beginning to tire.

- Offer praise and encouragement. Children are more likely to be successful if they are relaxed.

- Make sure that you are both comfortable and as free from distractions as possible. In school, the teacher should direct you to a suitable space, but do report back if there are any problems with the accommodation provided.

- Please do not comment upon the child's progress in individual reading diaries, but do convey any relevant observations to the class teacher either verbally or in the record book provided.

We hope this information will prove helpful. Please do not hesitate to consult the class teacher if you have any further questions regarding policy or practice.

BOOK REFERENCES

This list is designed to provide quick reference to all the books mentioned in the text, grouped according to topics described in the scheme of work. Some additional books have been included, where it was felt that they could be particularly useful.

Parodies
Clever Polly and the Stupid Wolf by Catherine Storr (Puffin)
Hairy Tales and Nursery Crimes by Michael Rosen (Armada)
It Shouldn't Happen to a Frog by Catherine Storr (Puffin)
Jim and the Beanstalk by Raymond Briggs (Picture Puffin)
Once Upon a Time by John Prater (Walker Books)
The Stinky Cheese Man and Other Fairly Stupid Tales by Jon Scieszka & Lane Smith (Puffin)
The True Story of the Three Little Pigs by a Wolf by Jon Scieszka (Viking)

Non-fiction
The Art Gallery: Stories by Philip. Wilkinson (Macmillan)
Kingfisher Kaleidoscopes (Kingfisher)
Think of an Eel by Karen Wallace (Read and Wonder series, Walker Books)
and other 'Read and Wonder' books
War Boy by Michael Foreman (Puffin)
The 'Whole Story' series (Viking Books)
The 'Wonderwise' series (Franklin Watts)
The Great Plague by Pam Robson (Macdonald Young Books)

Stories with familiar settings/coverage of 'issues'
Bill's New Frock by Anne Fine (Mammoth)
The Eighteenth Emergency by Betsy Byars (Puffin)
Flour Babies by Anne Fine (Puffin)
George Speaks by Dick King-Smith (Puffin)
Hacker by Malorie Blackman (Corgi)
Quirky Tales by Paul Jennings (Puffin)
The Turbulent Term of Tyke Tiler by Gene Kemp (Puffin)

Letters and Diaries
Anne Frank - Diary of a Young Girl by Anne Frank (Puffin)
Auntie Dot's Incredible Adventure Atlas by Eljay Yildirim (Collins)
The Ballad of Lucy Whipple by Karen Cushman (Macmillan)
The Jolly Postman by Janet and Allan Ahlberg (Heinemann)
The Last Polar Bears by Harry Horse (Puffin)
Letters From a Mouse by Herbie Brennan (Walker Books)
Little Wolf's Book of Badness by Ian Whybrow (Collins)
The Wreck of the Zanzarbar by Michael Morpurgo (Heinemann)

Historical stories
The Ballad of Lucy Whipple by Karen Cushman (Macmillan)
Children of Winter by Bertie Doherty (Mammoth)
The Naming of William Rutherford by Linda Kempton (Mammoth)
A Parcel of Patterns by Jill Paton Walsh (Puffin)
Smith by Leon Garfield (Puffin)
Shakespeare Stories by Leon Garfield (Puffin)
The Animated Tales by Leon Garfield (Heinemann)

Myths, Legends and Traditional Stories
The Adventures of Odysseus by Neil Philip (Orion)
Arthur - High King of Britain by Michael Morpurgo (Mammoth)
Black Ships Before Troy by Rosemary Sutcliff (Frances Lincoln Ltd)
Creation Stories from Around the World by Ann Pilling (Walker Books)
Greek Gods and Goddesses by Geraldine McCaughrean (Orchard Books)
King Arthur by Andrew Matthews (Orchard Books)
Orchard Book of Creation Stories by Margaret Mayo (Orchard Books)
Orchard Book of Greek Myths by Geraldine McCaughrean (Orchard Books)
Seasons of Splendour by Madhur Jaffrey (Puffin)
South, East, North and West by Michael Rosen (Walker Books)

Picture books
Each Peach, Pear, Plum by Janet and Allan Ahlberg (Penguin)
Grandfather's Pencil and the Room of Stories by Michael Foreman (Red Fox)
In Search of the Hidden Giant by Jeanne Willis and Ruth Brown (Red Fox)
Peter's Place by Sally Grindley, illustrated by Michael Foreman (Andersen Press)
Walk With a Wolf by Janni Howker (Walker Books)
When Jessie Came Across the Sea by Amy Hest (Walker Books)

Poetry Books
Crack Another Yolk compiled by John Foster (Oxford University Press)
The Orchard Book of Poems compiled by Adrian Mitchell (Orchard Books)
Please Mrs Butler by Allan Ahlberg (Puffin)
Heard it in the Playground by Allan Ahlberg (Puffin)
The Thirteen Secrets of Poetry by Adrian Mitchell (Macdonald)
This Poem Doesn't Rhyme edited by Gerard Benson (Puffin)
The Walker Book of Poetry for Children edited by Jack Prelutsky (Walker Books)
Wouldn't You Like to Know by Michael Rosen (Puffin)
You Tell Me by Michael Rosen (Puffin)
I Like This Poem edited by Kaye Webb (Puffin)

Miscellaneous fiction
The Demon Headmaster by Gillian Cross (Puffin)
Goodnight Mr Tom by Michelle Magorian (Puffin)
Green Smoke by Rosemary Manning (Puffin)
The Iron Man by Ted Hughes (Faber)
The Lion, the Witch and the Wardrobe by C.S. Lewis (Collins)
Real Life Stories edited by Betsy Byars (Kingfisher)
Rebecca's World by Terry Nation (Red Fox)
Treasure Island by Robert Louis Stevenson (Oxford University Press)

The author and publisher wish to thank the following for permission to reprint copyright material in this book:

Green Smoke by Rosemary Manning, reprinted by permission of Penguin Books Ltd.
Bill's New Frock by Anne Fine, reprinted by permission of Mammoth.
'The Listeners' by Walter de la Mare, reprinted by permission of the Literary Trustees of Walter de la Mare and The Society of Authors as their representative.
Letters from a Mouse by Herbie Brennan, reprinted by permission of Walker Books.
Little Wolf's Book of Badness by Ian Whybrow, reprinted by permission of Collins.
Anne Frank - The Diary of a Young Girl, reprinted by permission of Penguin Books Ltd.
The Ballad of Lucy Whipple, by Karen Cushman, reprinted by permission of Macmillan Children's Books.
The Wreck of the Zanzibar by Michael Morpurgo, reprinted by permission of Wm Heinemann.
Treasure Island by Robert Louis Stevenson, reprinted by permission of Oxford University Press.
The Last Polar Bears by Harry Horse, reprinted by permission of Penguin Books Ltd.

For details of further Belair publications,
please write to: Libby Masters,
BELAIR PUBLICATIONS LIMITED,
Albert House, Apex Business Centre,
Boscombe Road, Dunstable, LU5 4RL.

For sales and distribution in North America and South America,
INCENTIVE PUBLICATIONS,
3835 Cleghorn Avenue, Nashville, Tn 37215.
USA.

For sales and distribution in Australia
EDUCATIONAL SUPPLIES PTY LTD
8 Cross Street, Brookvale, NSW 2100.
Australia

For sales and distribution (in other territories)
FOLENS PUBLISHERS
Albert House, Apex Business Centre,
Boscombe Road, Dunstable, LU5 4RL.
United Kingdom.
E-mail: folens@folens.com